Managing IT Software Development Teams:
The relationship between the use of software development methodology, leadership style, and job satisfaction

Jodine Marie Burchell, PhD

M.S., University of Phoenix, 2004

A.A.S., Nashville State Technical Institute, 1997

B.B.A., Middle Tennessee State University, 1988

Table of Contents

List of Tables

List of Figures

Preface

Many information technology (IT) projects are managed with the use of software development methodologies (SDMs) as the project progresses through the systems development life cycle. However, some IT projects are managed without the use of SDMs. Currently, very little research focuses on SDM use and its effect on IT personnel. The problem addressed in this study was whether job satisfaction is influenced by the use of SDMs in IT projects. Job satisfaction is known to have an effect on voluntary turnover, which is very costly to organizations. The purpose of this quantitative study was to determine whether the use of SDMs in IT projects is associated with IT employees having higher overall job satisfaction and to examine the influence of leadership style for IT leaders who use SDMs compared to those who do not. The research questions addressed the relationship between SDM use, leadership style, and job satisfaction. The primary theoretical framework for the study was sociotechnical theory. The research methodology was a quantitative, correlational design utilizing a cross-sectional Internet-based survey that is descriptive in nature. Correlation and multiple regression analyses were used to test the hypotheses. Data were collected from 95 individuals who self-identified as belonging to a software development team. A Pearson product-moment analysis showed there was no significant relationship between SDM use and overall job satisfaction. A significant relationship was found between the 3 leadership styles and job satisfaction. Regression analysis indicated small differences when comparing models between SDM users and non-SDM users. The results of the study may affect social change and afford IT project leaders the ability to make better strategic decisions that could positively affect job satisfaction and reduce turnover intention.

Chapter 1: Introduction

The current business environment is increasingly globalized, knowledge based, and technology based (Marion, McKelvey, & Uhl-Bien, 2007). Organizational leaders must learn how to utilize all their assets, especially social, physical, and technological assets, to remain competitive. Technology has advanced rapidly, causing organizations to adapt constantly to remain connected to their customers and partners (Boban, Pozgaj, & Sertic, 2007). The role of information systems in organizations has evolved from the business support role in previous years to a more fundamental business driver where failure to evolve and adapt to new technologies may result in a decrease in the ability to remain competitive or to respond to new business opportunities. Although change is constant and market conditions may differ from week to week or even day to day, to survive and thrive, organizational leaders must consistently seek to create information systems that will be efficient and sufficiently customized to meet their needs (Boban et al., 2007). Thus, organizational leaders should be constantly aware of market trends and new technologies, evaluate their own current systems to ensure they are still effective, and be prepared to commit time and resources to information technology (IT) development.

IT projects and the development of information systems can be a requirement for any aspect of an organizational change. Improved or new systems can enhance communications, allow for knowledge sharing across departments, and provide for more efficient daily operations. Leaders of organizations have a better ability to utilize communication networks to offer its products and services to the public (Boban et al., 2007). However, introducing new technology into an organization is increasingly complex. IT development is usually a complicated and time-consuming endeavor. IT projects can take years to fully create and implement, and many technical and organizational components must be managed (Benbya & McKelvey, 2006).

In 2010, the Standish Group published the *Chaos Manifesto*, indicating that only 32% of IT projects studied were successful. The other 68% of IT projects studied were categorized as not successful, which ranged from failed and abandoned projects to projects challenged due to reasons such as scope and schedule slippage, mismanagement of project changes, inadequate management commitment, and failure to meet requirements (Frolick, Kloppenborg, & Tesch, 2007; Standish Group, 2010). In addition, when looking at the use of software development methodologies (SDMs) and their comparative success rates, for agile methods, 43% of the projects studied were successful compared to projects using the waterfall method, where only 26% were successful (Standish Group, 2010). According to the Standish Group's *Chaos Manifesto*, the top factors that led to the success of IT projects included executive management support, project management expertise, the use of formalized methodologies, and the adoption of agile processes.

Many IT projects include information systems development, which is also commonly referred to as *software development*. Software developers are concerned with meeting all the technical needs of IT projects and may not completely understand all the internal business processes (Avison & Fitzgerald, 2008). Business personnel are familiar with all the business processes and may not understand relevant technological issues. The coordination gap between these two areas must be closed, which requires a project leader who can manage the IT project phases appropriately from gathering the user requirements through completion of the project (Boban et al., 2007).

The phases of an information systems development project are referred to as the system development life cycle (SDLC). Theorists and practitioners differ on the exact phases of the SDLC, but in general the phases consist of planning, analysis, design, implementation, and maintenance (Huang, 2009). From a sociotechnical standpoint, IT project leaders must be able to manage both the technological and the social or organizational aspects as the project progresses through the phases of the SDLC (Bajec & Vavpotic, 2009). In many cases, multiple iterations of the SDLC may be involved to provide multiple deliverables. The larger and more complex the IT project, the more difficult it is for IT project leaders to manage efficiently and the more likely the project will become challenged or fail. Additionally, ineffective leadership causes the risk of project failure to increase and the IT manager's leadership style plays an important part in the outcome of the project (Kocheria & Korrapati, 2010).

Another factor in IT project management is whether the project should utilize an SDM, which may also be referred to as an information systems development methodology. SDMs are a means to achieve the development of information systems and may include tasks, techniques, procedures, guidelines, and tools (Avison & Fitzgerald, 2008). The list of SDMs is lengthy and has evolved over time, with agile processes being one of the more popular current methodologies (Livermore, 2008). However, many IT projects are managed without the use of SDMs, and their value in IT projects is a topic of controversy (Huisman & Iivari, 2006; Khalifa & Verner, 2000).

IT personnel or software developers have an important role in the success or failure of a project and may participate in multiple phases of the SDLC. The analyst is usually the IT professional who will translate user requirements into technical objectives. It is usually the software developer who has the technical training and knowledge to design and create the new system to meet the needs of the technical objectives (Huang, 2009). IT projects require knowledgeable, skilled IT personnel to be successful. According to SamGnanakkan (2010), excessive turnover can be detrimental to an organization's ability to remain technically viable and competitive. Replacing IT personnel can be costly as the monetary expense can be as high as 150% of an annual salary (Bliss, 2010) and the potential knowledge attrition may be priceless. Therefore, it is in the organization's best interest to have a full understanding of the factors that lead to increasing job satisfaction and decreasing voluntary turnover for IT personnel (SamGnanakkan, 2010). How these factors interact is the subject of important research in academia and for successful organizations. The findings of the current study provide valuable information concerning IT projects, how they are managed, and the relationship between SDM use, leadership style, and IT personnel job satisfaction.

Problem Statement

The problem addressed in the study was whether job satisfaction is influenced by the use of SDMs in IT projects. Most existing inquiry involved determining which SDM is more effective (D'Andrea, Gangadharan, Ivanyukovich, & Marchese, 2005; Hanafiah & Kasirun, 2007), examining its role in IT projects (Kawalek & Leonard, 1996; Kim, King, & Ratbe, 1999), improving developer adoption (R. Collins, Green, & Hevner, 2004; Hardgrave & Riemenschneider, 2002), or evaluating specific methodologies such as agile software development methodologies (Livermore, 2008; Mahapatra, Mangalaraj, & Nerur, 2005). Little research exists regarding the effect of SDMs on IT personnel (Cray, 2009).

Many IT projects are managed with the use of formal SDMs as the project progresses through the SDLC; however, some IT projects are managed without the use of SDMs at all. In addition, the project manager's leadership style can play an important part in the outcome of an IT project (Kocheria & Korrapati, 2010). Job dissatisfaction is an antecedent to voluntary turnover (Lambert, Hogan, & Barton, 2001), and high turnover can be very costly in organizations in terms of both the cost of hiring and training employees and the loss of knowledge (Kempaiah & Luftman, 2007). Inquiry into this topic may fill a gap in the research literature and advance understanding of the relationship between effectively managed IT projects and job satisfaction.

Background of the Study

The earliest formal computer applications or software development occurred in the 1960s with little help from formalized SDMs (Avison & Fitzgerald, 2003). Over time, new methodologies were developed and introduced, "focusing on the identification of phases and stages it was thought would improve the management of systems development and introduce discipline" (Avison & Fitzgerald, 2003, p. 79). The arguments in favor of using SDMs include the ability to break projects into coherent steps; the ability to facilitate better management control of the development process, allowing for assigning specific tasks to IT personnel based on skills; and standardization of the process overall (B. Fitzgerald, 1998). In terms of organizational benefits, SDMs provide an opportunity to allow for the better control of risks and the ability to manage time and costs more effectively (Avison & Fitzgerald, 2008).

The arguments against using SDMs are just as many and include instability due to the constantly changing market, inflexibility due to the difficulty in making changes during the development process, failure to keep documentation current, mismatches between the SDM and size and type of project, and the potential to focus on the SDM rather than software development and implementation (Avison & Fitzgerald, 2003). In more recent years and based on the evolution of technology, other SDMs are more flexible. These methods are referred to as agile processes and are characterized as being adaptable to continual change (Aydin, Harmsen, Stegwee, & van Slooten, 2005). Even with the evolution of SDMs to match the evolution of technological advances, many IT managers still do not use SDMs for their IT projects. In fact, in a study conducted in the United Kingdom, only 57% of IT systems development professionals surveyed utilized a formalized SDM (G. Fitzgerald, Philippides, & Probert, 1999).

Researchers have focused on the adoption and use of SDMs, specifically inquiring into the role of SDMs in IT projects (Kawalek & Leonard, 1996; Kim et al., 1999), which SDM is more effective (D'Andrea et al., 2005; Hanafiah & Kasirun, 2007), evaluations of specific methodologies (Livermore, 2008; Mahapatra et al., 2005), or improving developer adoption (R. Collins et al., 2004; Hardgrave & Riemenschneider,

2002). However, a review of the literature indicated very little research exists regarding which IT project leader's leadership style is more commonly associated with SDM use and, more important, whether the adoption of SDMs affects IT personnel and their job satisfaction level. The current study was designed to examine whether correlational relationships exist between formalized SDM use, leadership style, and job satisfaction.

Purpose of the Study

One purpose of the quantitative study was to determine whether the use of SDMs is associated with IT employees having higher job satisfaction. Another purpose was to examine the relationship of leadership style between IT managers who use SDMs in IT projects versus those who do not. Investigating the relationship between the variables SDM use, leadership style, and job satisfaction helped inform understanding regarding how IT personnel's job satisfaction is influenced by the use of SDMs in general and the role that leadership style plays as well. Given that information systems development is a complex endeavor for any organization and IT project leaders may or may not fully understand the influence of using SDMs in both a social and a technical sense, this information could be useful in any organization that utilizes information systems development to remain viable and competitive. In addition, findings from the study might help IT project leaders make better decisions regarding the development of strategies to manage difficult IT projects more effectively.

Significance of the Study

The significance of the study was in the premise that promoting the use of formalized SDMs paired with the appropriate leadership style relates to higher job satisfaction and ultimately leads to lower turnover rates for IT personnel in organizations. High turnover can be very costly in organizations, in terms of both the cost of hiring and training employees and the loss of knowledge. Although there is an abundance of research concerning topics relative to project success and SDMs, very little inquiry exists regarding how the use or nonuse of SDMs in IT projects affects IT personnel. The results have the potential to affect positive social change in the area of IT management by highlighting the relationship between SDM use, leadership style, and job satisfaction. The findings should provide management with information for developing strategies to successfully manage IT projects. In addition, the findings should provide management with knowledge regarding job satisfaction and reducing voluntary turnover in their organizations. Considering the Standish Group's findings that only 32% of the IT projects studied were successful (Standish Group, 2010) and many IT project leaders do not use formalized SDMs, the current study had the potential to provide organizations and IT project leaders with valuable information regarding the use of SDMs and their relationship to project success and job satisfaction for IT personnel.

Nature of the Study

The method of inquiry for the study was a correlational research design utilizing a cross-sectional Internet survey that was descriptive in nature. Correlational research involves collecting data and using correlational statistical techniques to determine if a relationship exists, and to what degree, between quantifiable variables (Simon, 2006). By utilizing an electronic survey, the nature of the quantitative correlational study was to determine whether a relationship existed between the independent variables and the dependent variable. The independent variables were SDM use and leadership style. The dependent variable was job satisfaction.

In addition to a quantitative correlational research design, qualitative methods including phenomenology, case study, and grounded theory were also considered. These qualitative methodologies tend to be used for context-rich research and utilize an inductively created theory and thus were not appropriate for the study. The quantitative design of the study was appropriate because there was a deductively created theory and a need to generalize the results of a sample across a population (Creswell & Plano Clark, 2007).

Most quantitative methods include either a survey or an experimental design. By utilizing a numeric study of trends or opinions, survey designs include a sample of a population and involve an attempt to generalize or make claims about that population (Creswell, 2009). One of the more important trends in recent years is the use of Internet-based surveys, which offer the advantage of cost and time savings as well as the opportunity to collect data from multiple organizations across a more geographically dispersed area (Singleton & Straits, 2010).

The study population included members of software development teams who have worked on a recent IT project involving software development. The team members could include analysts, software designers, programmers, IT quality assurance, or systems administrators. IT project leaders were not included in the study. Purposive sampling was the method used for choosing the sample of participants. Singleton and Straits (2010) indicated that purposive sampling is a method of sampling in which, based on his or her expertise, the researcher selects participants who are representative of the population.

The instruments for the study included Spector's (1985) Job Satisfaction Survey (JSS) and the Multifactor Leadership Questionnaire (MLQ 5X; Bass & Avolio, 1990). The dependent variable was job satisfaction, and the JSS was used to assess nine facets of job satisfaction, including overall job satisfaction (Spector, 1985). One of the independent variables was leadership style. The MLQ is one of the most widely used instruments to measure characteristics of transformational leadership. The most recent version of the MLQ (5X) has evolved since the original version and includes an assessment for all aspects of the full range of leadership model including transformational leadership, transactional leadership, and passive-avoidant leadership (Bass & Riggio, 2006). Both instruments are highly validated, so a pilot study was not required.

In addition, the Internet-based survey enabled the collection of information regarding whether each participant's IT project team utilized a formal SDM. Demographic data such as age, gender, and team size were collected. The leadership style and SDM-use data were used to determine if correlations exist between these variables and the dependent variable job satisfaction. Chapter 3 contains more in-depth information regarding the research methodology, sample, survey instrument, data collection, and data analysis procedures.

Theoretical Framework

The theoretical frameworks for the study included sociotechnical theory and adaptive structuration theory (AST). AST is an adaption by DeSanctis and Poole (1994) of Giddens's (1984) structuration theory that considers both the technological and the social aspects of the interactions of groups and organizations. Giddens developed the theory of structuration to explain how social systems should be conceptualized. According to Giddens, systems are organized social practices or relations reproduced among actors. Structures include the rules and resources that are considered properties of social systems. The *structuration* of systems refers to the duality of agents and structures and how the activities of actors who draw upon the rules and resources in their normal actions assist in producing and reproducing systems by their interactions across time and space (Giddens, 1984). Similarly, the concepts of AST expound on the nature of social structures within information technologies and their dual relationship whereby systems and structures create and recreate each other in an ongoing cycle (DeSanctis & Poole, 1994).

DeSanctis and Poole (1994) adapted Giddens's (1984) structuration theory due to the onset of advanced information technologies. In organization activities, researchers use AST to examine change from two viewpoints: (a) the types of structures provided by advanced technologies and (b) the structures that emerge from human action as agents interact with advanced technologies (DeSanctis & Poole, 1994). In AST, the nature of social structures within IT is explained, as well as the interaction process that occurs by their use. According to DeSanctis and Poole, "Technologies differ in the social structures they provide, and groups can adapt technologies in different ways, develop different attitudes towards them, and use them for social purposes" (p. 143). By identifying these processes and their effects, the complexity of organization–technology relationships is revealed and provides a better practical understanding of how humans and technology interact.

According to DeSanctis and Poole (1994), AST was designed with the influence of various theoretical approaches, including sociotechnical systems theory. Sociotechnical theory started as a research effort by the psychologist and social scientists at the Tavistock Institute of Human Relations to improve life for everyday working people and by associating human intelligence and skills with technology in an effort to revolutionize the way people do work (Mumford, 2006). Sociotechnical theory was also influenced by Bertalanffy's (1968) concepts of open systems. It is within the open-systems concept that the duality between work roles and technical structures is considered, as well as how they are part of one inclusive system (Mumford, 2006).

Sociotechnical theory has evolved over time to adapt to organizations that are more technology and information systems based. The sociotechnical perspective indicates that an organization consists of a technical subsystem and a social subsystem that will work effectively together if they are recognized as interdependent aspects of the whole system or organization (Clegg, 2000). The technical subsystem includes the "processes, tasks, and technology needed to perform inputs to outputs" (Bostrom & Heinen, 1977, p. 17). The social subsystem includes "the attributes of people (e.g., attitudes, skills, values), the relationships among people, reward systems, and authority structures" (Bostrom & Heinen, 1977, p. 17). Sena and Shani (1994) added that the social subsystem also includes relationships within groups and between groups. The outputs are created because of the interaction between these two subsystems. In addition, many of the attributes of the social subsystem also relate to job satisfaction and the antecedents of IT turnover intention (Aurum & Ghapanchi, 2011). Organizations whose leaders seek change using information systems must have IT project leaders who can manage the subsystems in an integrated form.

Research Questions and Hypotheses

The quantitative, correlational study involved examining the relationship, if any, between SDM, leadership style, and job satisfaction for IT personnel. The research questions were as follows:

1. What is the relationship, if any, between formal SDM use and overall job satisfaction?
2. What is the relationship, if any, between leadership style of leaders who are SDM users versus leaders who are non-SDM users and overall job satisfaction?

Based on these research questions, the hypotheses were as follows:

$H1_0$: There is no relationship between formal SDM use and overall job satisfaction for IT software development team members.

$H1_a$: There is a relationship between formal SDM use and overall job satisfaction for IT software development team members.

$H2_0$: There is no difference in the relationship between leadership style of leaders who use SDM versus leaders who do not use SDM and overall job satisfaction for IT software development team members.

$H2_a$: There is a difference in the relationship between leadership style of leaders who use SDM versus leaders who do not use SDM and overall job satisfaction for IT software development team members.

Definition of Terms

Many key terms used throughout the study appear repeatedly and can be used interchangeably. Each of the terms is defined to reduce confusion or ambiguity.

Agile processes (also referred to as *agile project management*): A set of values, principles, and practices that assist project teams in a constantly changing environment. The core values address the need to build agile, adaptable products and the need to create agile, adaptable development teams (Highsmith, 2004, p. 17).

Information systems: A set of interrelated components that collect, manipulate, store, and disseminate data and information and provide a feedback mechanism to meet an objective (Reynolds & Stair, 2010, p. 4).

Information technology (IT): Any computer-based tool that people use to work with information and to support the information and information-processing needs of an organization (Cegielski & Rainer, 2007, p. 7).

Job satisfaction: How people feel about their jobs and different aspects of their jobs (Spector, 1997, p. 2).

Leadership: A process whereby an individual influences a group of individuals to achieve a common goal (Northouse, 2004, p. 3).

Leadership style: The manner by which leaders express specific behaviors. Autocratic, consultative, and democratic are some examples (Aditya & House, 1997, p. 451).

Project managers (also referred to as *IT project leaders*): Persons who manage a project with particular emphasis on schedules and resources (Avison & Fitzgerald, 2008, p. 11).

Software developer (also referred to as a *programmer* or *systems developer*): IT personnel who code and develop a system in a computer programming language (Avison & Fitzgerald, 2008, p. 11).

Software development methodology (*SDM*; also referred to as information systems development methodology): A recommended means to achieve the development, or part of the development, of information systems based on a set of rationales and an underlying philosophy that supports, justifies, and makes coherent such a recommendation for a particular context. The recommended means usually includes the identification of phases, procedures, tasks, rules, techniques, guidelines, documentation, and tools (Avison & Fitzgerald, 2008, p. 568).

Systems development life cycle (*SDLC*; also referred to as software development life cycle): A series of stages including feasibility study, system investigation, systems analysis, systems design, implementation, and review and maintenance, used together in the process of creating information systems (Avison & Fitzgerald, 2008, p. 31).

Voluntary turnover: A case in which organizational leaders do not want an employee to quit and the employee wants to (Ali & Baloch, 2010, p. 41).

Assumptions

The design of the study included some basic assumptions. The first assumption was that the participants would understand and answer the survey questions truthfully. Another assumption was that the participants would self-identify correctly as being a member of a software development team and that only those who meet the criteria will take the survey. Potential participants received an e-mail that explained the survey and the criteria for participation. One assumption was that members of the software development team would have knowledge of which SDM is used, if any, for the specified IT project. In addition, it was assumed that the SDM utilized by the IT project leader, if any, was actually followed by the team members. The final assumption was that the sampling methods utilized for the study would allow the Internet survey to reach an adequate cross section of the software development population.

Scope and Delimitations

The scope of the quantitative, correlational study involved the use of an Internet-based electronic survey to examine the relationship between SDM use, leadership style, and job satisfaction. The target population included self-identified members of software development teams who participated in a recent IT project involving software development. A delimitation of the study included the fact that the survey dispersion does not control for types and sizes of organizations, including those in the private sector versus nongovernmental agencies. Having an appropriate sample size and validated instruments helped ensure the results were generalized to the population; however, a study on a specific industry or on governmental agencies versus the private sector may produce different results.

Limitations

A limitation of the study involved its correlational nature. One of the disadvantages of using correlation techniques is an association may be detected but causality is not determined (Singleton & Straits, 2010). Thus, while a statistical analysis using correlational methods will provide information regarding the relationships between SDM use, leadership style, and job satisfaction, a claim that SDM use or a specific leadership style causes higher job satisfaction cannot be made.

Summary

Chapter 1 contained an overall introduction to the study, highlighting a common predicament for many IT project leaders. Most IT projects require management of the software development process as it progresses through the systems development life cycle. Some IT projects are managed with the use of SDMs and some are not. Although there is much research regarding different aspects of SDMs, there is little research on the effect of SDM use on IT personnel or which leadership style of IT project leaders is more commonly associated with SDM use. The problem was reflected in the research questions and hypotheses. In addition, chapter 1 included the theoretical foundation for the study; the nature, purpose, and significance of the study; and the assumptions, scope, delimitations, and limitations. The introductory information presented in chapter 1 helped to lay a foundation for the study and provided insight into subsequent chapters.

Chapter 2 will include a literature review essay that is relevant for the key concepts of the study, including SDMs, IT project management, leadership, and job satisfaction. Two theoretical frameworks, AST and sociotechnical theory, will be addressed and related to the key concepts of the study. Chapter 3 will include a discussion on the use of a correlational design for the study. An explanation of the methodology will be presented, including why it was appropriate for answering the research questions. Chapter 3 will also include a discussion of the setting, sample, survey instrument, and data collection methods.

Chapter 4 provides a detailed report of how the study was conducted, how the data collection was performed, and the data analysis techniques used. Descriptive statistics were used to create a demographic profile of the participants. A Pearson product-moment correlation was performed to test the hypotheses and to answer the research questions. Chapter 5 provides an interpretation of the research findings. Additionally, chapter 5 provides an explanation of the limitations of the study, recommendations for action, and suggestions for future research. The chapter concludes with a discussion of implications for social change.

Chapter 2: Literature Review

According to the Standish Group (2010), only 32% of IT projects studied were successful. An IT project success survey designed to assess project success under four separate SDM paradigms indicated that the current IT project success rate range is between 47 and 61% (Ambler, 2010). In addition, the 2010 study indicated that projects using agile methods and other iterative methods have 60 to 61% success rates, whereas projects with no SDM use or that use older noniterative methods have 47-49% success rates (Ambler, 2010). In spite of the apparent increase in IT project success and the higher success rates in projects utilizing agile and iterative SDMs, 60% of organizations do not use SDMs at all (B. Fitzgerald, 1998). Managing software development projects without the use of any SDM will increase the probability of project failure (Pressman, 2007) or may result in a software crisis as indicated by the project running over time or budget; inefficient, low-quality software; or software deliverability issues (Kaur & Sengupta, 2010).

A review of literature indicated considerable research and discussion around the technical aspects of IT projects and the effects of SDM use on project success and user satisfaction; however, little information is available on the relationship of SDM use and job satisfaction for IT personnel. Software developers usually have the technical training and knowledge to design and create a new system to meet technical objectives (Huang, 2009). IT projects require knowledgeable, skilled IT personnel to be successful. Excessive turnover can be detrimental to the ability of an organization to remain technically viable and competitive (SamGnanakkan, 2010). Replacing IT personnel can be costly, as the monetary expense of replacing IT employees can be as high as 150% of their annual salary (Bliss, 2010) and the potential knowledge attrition may be debilitating to an organization.

Many different ways exist for researchers and theorists to classify leadership styles. Using the components of the full model of transformational leadership as leadership styles, the research spans many different topics and subject areas. The literature indicates a link exists between transformational leadership and individual follower performance, and consequently, job satisfaction (Bono, Dzieweczynski, & Purvanova, 2006; Colquitt & Piccolo, 2006). A link also exists between transformational leadership and innovation and project team success (Bass & Riggio, 2006; Bono et al., 2006). In addition, the concepts of SDMs and transformational leadership are both underpinned by sociotechnical theory and the idea that IT project leadership is more likely to be successful if a leader and his or her leadership style fit with the need to manage both the human aspects and the technological process involved in software development projects (Guinan & Sawyer, 1998).

The purpose of the current study was to examine the relationship between SDM use and leadership style of SDM users versus nonusers and job satisfaction for IT personnel. The purpose of the literature review was to provide an in-depth examination of each of the topics, including how they are interrelated as well as how related theories were used to inform the study. Although the challenge of leading IT projects, organizational adoption, and use of SDMs was apparent throughout the literature, understanding the issue around SDM use specific to its effect on IT personnel is complex and required examination from multiple perspectives.

Chapter 2 contains an analysis of germinal and current research for the topics involved in the study. The first section includes information on SDMs, their history, and the factors influencing their use. The next section contains a description of sociotechnical theory and AST and how the theories underpinned and informed the concepts of the study. The third section includes an examination of leadership style and the components of transformational leadership. The concepts and literature regarding motivation, job satisfaction, and turnover intention are examined in the fourth section, and the final section contains a summary of information from the literature.

Strategy for Searching the Literature

The primary sources for the literature review included journal articles from peer-reviewed journals, dissertations, professional websites, and germinal books. Journal articles were extracted from the Walden University library search engines and databases, including Sage Publications, ProQuest, Ovid, IEEE, EBSCOhost, Science Direct, and ERIC. Database searches included the following key words and phrases: *software developer, software development, information systems development, job satisfaction, motivation, leadership style, software development methodologies, SDLC, software development life cycle, agile, agile methods, voluntary turnover, socio-technical, sociotechnical, structuration,* and *adaptive structuration.* The original database searches utilizing these keywords or phrases provided approximately 220 journal articles. The number of articles that contributed to the study was approximately 150.

The History of Software Development

The earliest formal computer applications of the 1960s were created and implemented without the use of systematic SDMs (Avison & Fitzgerald, 2008). The emphasis for software development projects was placed on the technological abilities of the software developers rather than their softer skills such as the ability to communicate with users and understand business processes (Avison & Fitzgerald, 2003). As a result, many software programs and systems development did not fully meet the needs of the users (Avison & Fitzgerald, 2008). In the 1970s and early 1980s, the focus shifted to identifying the phases and stages, known as the SDLC, to more effectively manage software development projects (Huang, 2009). As shown in Figure 1, the methodology of the time was called the *waterfall method* and was characterized by its linear nature, where one phase was to be completed before the next could be started. This approach soon proved to have several limitations, including inflexibility, user dissatisfaction, documentation issues, and application backlog (Avison & Fitzgerald, 2003).

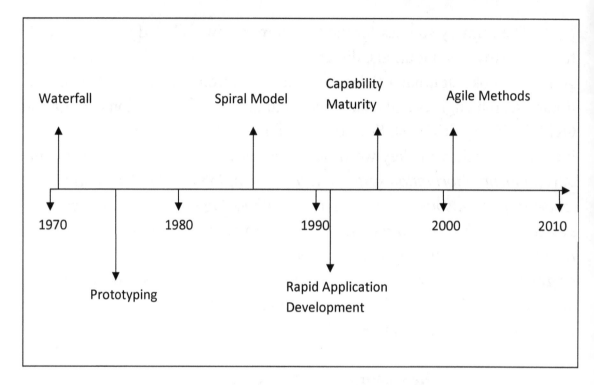

Figure 1. Historical timeline of software development methodologies.

According to Dahiya and Jain (2010), there have been considerable paradigm shifts in the field of software development since the 1960s. Newer approaches were developed to better manage software development projects and were referred to as SDMs. The SDMs were "a collection of phases, procedures, rules, techniques, tools, documentation, management, and training used to develop a system" (Avison & Fitzgerald, 2003, p. 80). Some of the new methodologies that followed the waterfall method became more iterative and flexible in nature. With each shift in the way practitioners approach software development, there were also new ways of viewing problems and new strengths and weaknesses to consider (Dahiya & Jain, 2010). Avison and Fitzgerald (2003) classified these newer methodologies into broad categories, including the following:

1. Structured: The concepts of structured, top-down programming were applied to analysis and design tasks and allowed for the representation of complex processes.
2. Data-oriented: The focus was on data as the key element in software development and entity modeling as an important technique.
3. Prototyping: The creation of a representation of the system allowing users to see the potential end product and make comments.
4. Object-oriented: The identification of objects, attributes, and classes to help provide the theoretical benefits of reuse and inheritance.
5. Participative: The focus is on involvement of the users and stakeholders throughout the process.
6. Strategic: The focus is on the planning and development of an IT strategy to support the goals of the business.
7. Systems: Utilizes a holistic view that addresses human activity systems that reach beyond the single-application boundaries of a system.

These categories are only one example of the different classifications of SDMs that have been created over time.

By the late 1990s, there was some reworking of SDMs to include agile methods in answer to the increasingly dynamic business environment in organizations (Mahapatra et al., 2005). Agile SDMs were characterized by utilizing iterative software development to be better able to adapt to changing business requirements (Livermore, 2008) and to handle the increased complexity of current software products (Brinkkemper, Jansen, Jaspers, & Vlaandered, 2010). Although SDMs had evolved over time, some organizations were questioning the effectiveness of SDMs, and some had entirely abandoned using them altogether (Avison & Fitzgerald, 2003).

The Fundamentals of SDMs

An SDM is a means for developing information systems. An SDM is also a strategy that IT leaders use for computer-based software development that includes a framework for addressing the sequence of development tasks as well as the techniques to complete each task (Fields, Gibson, Ranier, & Roberts, 1998). According to Fields et al. (1998), SDMs are important because they are teachable, they provide consistency, they require deliverables that may be quality checked, and they have an engineering-like discipline. Although many researchers and practitioners believe in the importance of SDM use in IT projects, little research supports the claim (Cray, 2009; Fields et al., 1998).

According to Millet and Pinto (1999), two of the components in the creation of software and use of SDMs involve process management and human management. Process management involves the key components of a successful implementation, including organizing the project and its critical success factors, whereas human management refers to the IT leader's ability to manage a software development team for maximum performance (Millet & Pinto, 1999). IT leaders cannot focus on one component rather than the other, as both are required for successful IT implementation.

Guinan and Sawyer (1998) introduced a multiperspective view to developing software that included a production perspective and social processes. The production perspective involves the focus on the project and how individuals should work. Methodologies, techniques, and tools are utilized to manage the project better and support the efforts of the software developers. The social process involves examining how developers work together in teams to build software and includes intergroup coordination and communication. Guinan and Sawyer examined the effects of these perspectives on software quality and performance. The findings indicated that although both production and social processes are needed in software development projects, the social processes tend to be a better predictor of the performance of software development teams than the production perspective (Guinan & Sawyer, 1998). These findings are only slightly different from Millet and Pinto's (1999) assertions that process management and human management are equally important in IT projects.

Analysis of the Evolution of Software Methodologies

As shown in Figure 1, the first formally developed SDM was the waterfall approach. Royce (1970) created a germinal work outlining the basic structure of the SDLC. The SDLC, also referred to as the waterfall approach, was created with general steps or phases for software development, including collecting system requirements, analysis, system design, coding, testing, implementation, and maintenance (Avison & Fitzgerald, 1995). Each of the steps has specific entry and exit criteria (Amudha, 2010), and as shown in Figure 2, each of the steps of the SDLC are meant to be completed before the next step begins (Avison & Fitzgerald, 1995).

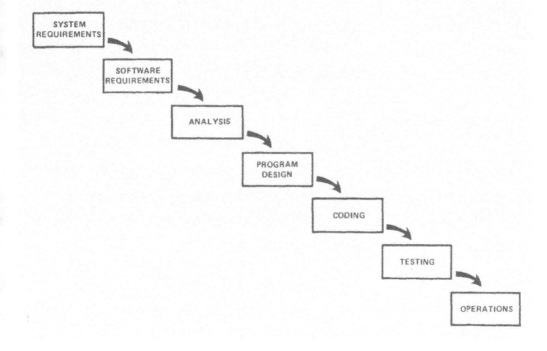

Figure 2. Steps of the software development life cycle (or waterfall method).
From "Managing the Development of Large Software Systems" by W. Royce, 1970, *Proceedings of the IEEE WESCON, 26,* p. 329. Copyright 1970 by the Institute of Electrical and Electronics Engineers. Reprinted with permission (see Appendix A).

One of the criticisms of the waterfall approach is its linear nature (Mahapatra et al., 2005). Royce (1970) maintained that, under optimal conditions, his model could be iterative if the interaction between the steps is confined to successive steps; however, Royce also indicated that "design iterations are never confined to the successive step" (p. 330). Royce called for emphasis on the design stage to ensure a complete and accurate design before moving to the next step.

One of the criticisms of earlier methodologies such as the waterfall method is that a large effort is needed on the front end of the project, especially the planning phase, and as much as half of the project's resources may be expended before any programming occurs (Cervone, 2011). According to theorists and practitioners, even though Royce attempted to take steps to make his model more dynamic, the waterfall approach falls short unless IT project leaders use it correctly (Avison & Fitzgerald, 1995). Avison and Fitzgerald (1995) advocated for viewing the process as one that involves technology, developers, and users rather than a purely technical process. In addition, IT leaders should manage the process well to recognize deviations from the original plan, assign adequate resources, and view the process as flexible rather than rigid so that it may be used somewhat iteratively (Avison & Fitzgerald, 1995). Other potential weaknesses of the waterfall method include its failure to meet the needs of management, instability, inflexibility, and being too simplistic to meet the complex needs of many organizations (Avison & Fitzgerald, 1995).

Prototyping. In many cases, during the requirements collection phase of the SDLC, there is a disconnect between the IT person gathering information who may lack understanding in the business application area and the user who may provide information "without a clear understanding of the overall concept of this system, its objectives and functions" (Slusky, 1987, p. 380). In response to the phenomenon, prototyping was introduced in an effort to provide a working version of the system early in its development. While there are differing types of prototypes, one of the popular types is incremental prototyping, which allows for the building of a system one section or one piece of the design at a time. With each version, the user accepts the design until the new system is built (Hekmatpour & Ince, 1987).

According to Hekmatpour and Ince (1987), even though it may be seen as an extension of the waterfall approach, prototyping includes stages of its own, including the establishment of objectives, function selection, prototype construction, and prototype evaluation. One of the advantages of utilizing prototyping is the increase in communication between the systems designers and users earlier in the development process, which means there is a higher user buy-in and greater potential of reduced issues in the finished product (Slusky, 1987). An increase in user–designer communication through prototyping provides a feasible method of validating specifications and a reduction of risk (Royce, 1992). One of the potential problems associated with prototyping involves using prototyping too quickly in the process, which may result in an inadequate set of requirements (Hekmatpour & Ince, 1987). Additionally, there may be difficulty due to the unknown number of prototypes needed, which may require tighter control of planning and other areas by IT project leaders (Dearnley, Mayhew, & Worsley, 1989; Slusky, 1987).

Spiral model. According to Boehm (1988), many of the deficiencies of the waterfall approach were addressed over time by the addition of extensions as well as various revisions and refinements. However, continued difficulties inspired theorists to create models that utilize a risk-driven approach to the software development process rather than a code-driven process (Boehm, 1988). As shown in Figure 3, the creation of Boehm's spiral model allowed for the use of incremental phases and prototyping in software development, especially for larger, more complex IT projects. Each typical cycle of the spiral model begins with identification of the objectives of this portion of the system, implementation alternatives, potential constraints, evaluation of alternatives to objectives, identification of risks, and strategy for resolving risks. These tasks occur at the beginning of each cycle and are repeated throughout the process of creating the system (Boehm, 1988). The objectives of each cycle generally coincide with the phases of the waterfall approach and prototyping, including gathering requirements, refining requirements, developing prototypes at the appropriate stages, completing requirement specifications, completing the design document, and building and testing the final product (Nelson, Nute, & Rodjak, 1996). After each the objectives has been completed, additional cycle tasks include gathering and reviewing results, planning the next cycle, and committing to the next plan and cycle (Wolff, 1989).

Boehm (1988) asserted that the spiral model allowed for the development of specifications in a less formal manner, the use of multiple prototyping events such as risk reduction, and the ability to do rework without a large amount of risk involved. One of the disadvantages is that spiral models tend to work well for internal software development, which is known to be more flexible and allows for incremental implementations rather than contract development where the user usually needs specific deliverables on a specific time schedule (Boehm, 1988). Oriogun (2002) contended that the spiral model is appropriate for commercial software because each increment produces a working version; therefore, with each release, new features may also be released. Additionally, one of the potential shortcomings of the spiral model is that it calls for IT project leaders who are proficient at measuring risk (Oriogun, 2002). If a major risk is not identified and managed, then there may be potential problems.

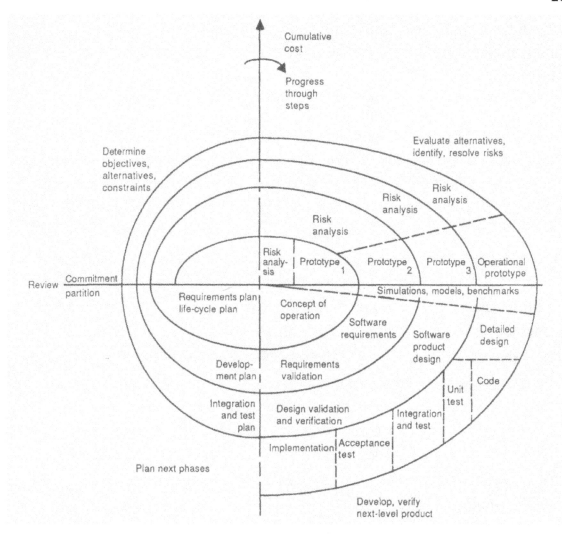

Figure 3. Spiral model of the software process. From "A Spiral Model of Software Development and Enhancement" by B. Boehm, 1988, *Computer, 21*(5), p. 64. Copyright 1988 by IEEE. Reprinted with permission (see Appendix A).

Rapid application development. In keeping with the evolving theme of iterative software development and incremental deliverables, Martin (1991) created rapid application development (RAD) as "an integrated set of techniques, guidelines, and tools that facilitate deploying a customer's software needs within a short period of time" (as cited in Gottesdiener, 1995, p. 28). According to Gottesdiener (1995), RAD provides deliverables that have evolved through the development process based on feedback and in prioritized chunks, rather than one deliverable at the end of software development. The system is built iteratively and the focus is on developing incremental prototypes utilizing a cycle of inspection, discussion, and amendment until the system is complete and the user is happy (Berger & Beynon-Davies, 2009).

Rather than focusing on steps or phases, the focus in RAD is on delivery cycles defined by an end date utilizing the concept of a timebox (Gottesdiener, 1995). In RAD, *timeboxing* is part of a control process that gives scope to the project by using specific, negotiated deadlines (Beynon-Davies & Holmes, 2002). Gottesdiener (1995) noted that timeboxing is an important part of RAD because it is a mechanism that allows for the ability to control resources and forces team members to be cognizant of customer priorities and to focus on planning project components by short time frames rather than tasks and activities. Beynon-Davies and Holmes (2002) maintained that small development teams of four to eight persons characterize RAD teams, with both users and developers having the authority to make design decisions. In addition, the team members must have all the skills necessary to complete the job, a high level of cohesiveness, and a high level of interactivity (Beynon-Davies & Holmes, 2002), which means RAD may not be optimal in organizational cultures that are hierarchical in nature.

One of the shortcomings of RAD is the need for good tool support such as fourth-generation programming languages, graphical user interfaces, computer-aided software engineering tools, and relational databases (Beynon-Davies & Holmes, 2002). RAD would likely not work well for old mainframes and programming languages that are not prone to rapid development. In addition, RAD is not optimal for projects that have a high level of complexity, large-scale projects, and company-wide databases (Berger & Beynon-Davies, 2009; Beynon-Davies & Holmes, 2002).

Capability maturity model. Personnel at the Software Engineering Institute at Carnegie Mellon University created the capability maturity model (CMM) for the U.S. Department of Defense (Avison & Fitzgerald, 2008). According to Avison and Fitzgerald (2008), the CMM is not exactly a SDM, but rather it is a framework designed to help improve software processes in organizations by moving from chaotic ad-hoc software development to "more disciplined software processes in a staged approach" (p. 553). CMM allows for defining and establishing procedures so that software development practices are repeatable and able to be standardized (Ashrafi, 2003; Avison & Fitzgerald, 2008).

CMM has five process maturity levels specified by 18 key process areas (Ashrafi, 2003). Avison and Fitgerald (2008) noted that key process areas are items such as requirements management, software quality assurance, software project planning, and quantitative process management that IT leaders must focus on to achieve a particular maturity level. The five maturity levels of CMM include initial, repeatable, defined, managed, and optimizing (Ashrafi, 2003).

Avison and Fitzgerald (2008) maintained that CMM Level 1 is characterized as having chaotic crisis-based software development with few repeatable processes. Level 1 is the maturity level where many organizations without SDMs exist. As organizations adopt sound software development management practices and are able to implement well-defined practices for planning, estimating, tracking costs, scheduling, goal setting, becoming measured and predictable, and achieving continuous process improvement, then they will move up to higher levels of maturity (Avison & Fitzgerald, 2008).

While CMM has been adopted as an industry standard and has been utilized by such organizations as General Motors, Boeing, Motorola, and Lockheed Martin, just like any SDM or frameworks for improving systems development, the CMM is not without some criticisms (Avison & Fitzgerald, 2008). Eterovic and Guerrero (2004) noted that many organizations believe that formal software process improvement models such as the CMM are too expensive and complex for small organizations and not applicable to small development teams. However, in a case study of a small company that successfully implemented CMM as a software process improvement initiative, Eterovic and Guerrero discovered that the fact that the development team was small rather than large allowed for full participation and commitment to the process.

Another criticism of CMM is that it relates to the particular view of software development that an engineering approach is best (Avison & Fitzgerald, 2008). According to Avison and Fitzgerald (2008), the engineering approach is based on a manufacturing or product-building view of software development. Some theorists contended that software development can be conceptually different from a product mass production and to view it as such causes one to miss the complex issues of software development (Avison & Fitzgerald, 2008). In practical terms, CMM may be more appropriate; where the requirements are narrowly defined and scoped, the culture is similar to a manufacturing environment, the processes are fairly predictable, and the primary problem or issue does not involve the human element (Avison & Fitzgerald, 2008, p. 558).

Agile methods. Agile methods were conceptualized based on a need for a more evolutionary approach to programming. According to Mahapatra et al. (2005), software development is a complex activity with a high degree of variability and is characterized by rapidly changing tools caused by the diversity and unpredictability of people involved in the software development process. Whereas traditional methods tend to be linear in nature, process-centric, and partially iterative, agile methods are more people-centric, evolutionary, flexible, and collaborative in nature (Mahapatra et al., 2005). According to Cervone (2011), the focus of older SDMs is on the software development process itself, whereas the principles of agile methods are geared to make sense in a project development environment.

As shown in Figure 4, many differences exist between traditional and agile methods, including fundamental assumptions and management style. According to Mahapatra et al. (2005), the fundamental assumption of traditional SDMs is that "systems are fully specifiable, predictable, and can be built through meticulous and extensive planning" (p. 75). Conversely, the fundamental assumption of agile methods is that "high-quality, adaptable software can be developed by small teams using the principles of continuous design improvement and testing based on rapid feedback and change" (Mahapatra et al., 2005, p. 75). Agile methods can involve many different submethodologies, including Extreme Programming, SCRUM, Adaptive Software Development, and Crystal (Amudha, 2010). These software methodologies all utilize principles of agile methods, including incremental releases intended to increase productivity, short iterative cycles of development, collaborative decision making, and self-organizing teams (Mahapatra et al., 2005).

	Traditional	Agile
Fundamental Assumptions	Systems are fully specifiable, predictable, and can be built through meticulous and extensive planning.	High-quality, adaptive software can be developed by small teams using the principles of continuous design improvement and testing based on rapid feedback and change.
Control	Process centric	People centric
Management Style	Command-and-control	Leadership-and-collaboration
Knowledge Management	Explicit	Tacit
Role Assignment	Individual—favors specialization	Self-organizing teams—encourages role interchangeability
Communication	Formal	Informal
Customer's Role	Important	Critical
Project Cycle	Guided by tasks or activities	Guided by product features
Development Model	Life cycle model (Waterfall, Spiral, or some variation)	The evolutionary-delivery model
Desired Organizational Form/Structure	Mechanistic (bureaucratic with high formalization)	Organic (flexible and participative encouraging cooperative social action)
Technology	No restriction	Favors object-oriented technology

Figure 4. Traditional versus agile software development. From "Challenges of Migrating to Agile Methodologies" by R. Mahapatra, G. Mangalaraj, and S. Nerur, 2005, *Communications of the ACM, 48*(5), p. 75. Copyright 2005 by ACM. Reprinted with permission.

Aken (2008) contended that many IT failures are attributed to the methodology used or the lack of a methodology. One of the advantages of using agile methods is that they produce deliverables incrementally, which allows for quickly generated value and feedback received more quickly, which allows for the detection of problems earlier. Another advantage is that agile methods call for establishing clear goals and objectives, which is one of the more difficult aspects of software development (Aken, 2008). An important advantage of agile methods is its people orientation due to the importance placed on communication, collaboration, and having a team that works well together (Avison & Fitzgerald, 2008). Agile methods have also been advocated as an appropriate SDM when there is a need for high creativity and innovation in organizations that need to thrive in a more globalized, competitive marketplace (Conboy & Morgan, 2011).

According to Avison and Fitzgerald (2008), some criticisms indicated that agile methods may not be applicable in certain environments, including those with collocated development teams, large development teams, and development using subcontractors or outsourcing. In addition, agile methods may not be appropriate for safety-critical domains and very large or complex systems. In some cases, practitioners may question whether an agile method's emphasis is too focused on handling change rather than following a well-developed plan and too focused on creating software rather than on ensuring documentation (Avison & Fitzgerald, 2008). Agile methods tend to be viewed as being more efficient than older methodologies; however, they lack long-term planning capability (Hannan, 2011). In response to these criticisms, some research has indicated that agile methods will evolve to include the combination of agile and plan-driven approaches (Baskerville, Madsen, & Pries-Heje, 2011).

Factors in SDM Implementation

Even as software languages and computer technology have evolved over time and have improved to keep up with organizational technological needs, new improved SDMs have also been introduced to help IT leaders manage projects. According to B. Fitzgerald (1998), 60% of the organizations studied do not use SDMs. The factors that affect implementing an SDM can vary from study to study. According to Fields et al. (1998), key areas that companies have to address include overall organization support of the SDM transition, functional management support, components of the SDM transition, the use of models, developer support, which method to use, and external support such as consultants. Popular methodology selection criteria may include "project time, clarity of user requirements, familiarity with technology, system complexity, system reliability, and schedule visibility" (Ahmar, 2010, p. 144). Consequently, factors in choosing a methodology can vary from organization to organization.

Some of the reasons for adopting SDMs include the ability to accurately record user requirements, the ability to monitor the progress of the team better, the ability to identify and make changes earlier in the process, and the creation of systems within cost and time constraints (Avison & Fitzgerald, 1995). In addition, SDMs allow for the utilization of a framework to take advantage of techniques and resources at the appropriate time in an IT project as well as the potential to standardize the software development process better (B. Fitzgerald, 1998). In a study that looked to the software developer's role in SDM acceptance, the critical factors involved the extent to which a methodology is universally applicable, confidence in the method, the degree of developer's experience, codetermination in the software development process, and how the SDM is introduced to the organization and the team (Hansen, Jacobsen, & Kautz, 2004).

With the more recent introduction of agile methods to the software development community, researchers still show reluctance to use SDMs and include factors such as lack of training, management involvement, access to external sources, and corporation size (Livermore, 2008). Research includes numerous factors involved in the implementation of SDMs, including those at the organizational level, the leader level, and the software developer level. There has also been a recent interest in the examination of organizational culture factors and the deployment of agile methods (Iivari & Iivari, 2011). Successful adoption of an SDM requires not only meeting technology requirements but also taking the needs of IT personnel into consideration (Hansen et al., 2004; Livermore, 2008).

Two specific aspects of nonadoption include the claim that SDMs are not tailored to meet specific project and organizational needs and that SDMs do not fit well with the social needs of a development team or the organization (Bajec & Vavpotic, 2009). In many cases, the SDM may be technically suited for a project, but not socially appropriate for the team, or vice versa. The result of this problem may mean that developers resist using the SDM. To address this issue, Bajec and Vavpoptic (2009) created an approach for evaluating both the technical and the social suitability of an SDM.

Another aspect of nonadoption includes the perceptions of the SDM by software developers. In many cases, software developers may feel that by introducing an SDM, they are losing control of the software development process (R. Collins et al., 2004), which was especially true for software developers who felt that "software development is an ad hoc combination of technical skills and individualized artistry" (R. Collins et al., 2004, p. 124). In their study, R. Collins et al. (2004) determined that when software developers are given some control in the choice and implementation of SDMs, they are much more likely to be satisfied with the SDM and much more likely to support its use. These findings indicated that IT project leaders have to involve the software developers in the process of using SDMs to provide a better assurance of their success.

In a study designed to examine adoption intentions, Davis, Hardgrave, and Riemenschneider (2002) found that the drivers include whether an organizational mandate to use SDMs exists, the compatibility of the SDM with the work performed, and the opinions of supervisors and coworkers regarding the use of SDMs. The practical value of these findings provides some insight into how IT leaders will need to develop strategies to introduce new SDMs to a software development team and increase adoption to avoid expending time and money into methodologies that are not used or effective (Davis et al., 2002).

It is apparent from the literature that adoption or implementation issues for SDMs may involve the organizational, upper management, IT project leader, or software developer level. In addition to the information presented above, relevant research on the drivers of SDM acceptance and implementation is varied and includes topics such as the perceived quality of the methodology, perceptions of challenges or obstacles, and perceived usefulness (Duggan, Hale, Hale, Kacmar, & McManus, 2009); influences by support of supervisors, peers, and clients (Leonard-Barton, 1987); an organizational culture that is hierarchical toward security, order, and routinization (Huisman & Iivari, 2007); and software developers' predisposition based on creative style (Gallivan, 2003).

Sociotechnical Theory

Historically, sociotechnical theory was influenced by Bertalanffy's (1968) concepts of open systems. Within the open-systems concept, the duality between work roles and technical structures is considered, as well as how they are part of one inclusive system (Mumford, 2006). The sociotechnical perspective maintains that an organization is made up of a technical subsystem and a social subsystem that will work effectively together if they are recognized as interdependent aspects of the whole system or organization (Clegg, 2000). The technical subsystem uses technology processes and tasks to transform inputs to output or in the process of software development (Bostrom & Heinen, 1977). The social subsystem includes the relationships among people, the attitudes and skills of people, the reward systems, and the structures of authority (Bostrom & Heinen, 1977). Additionally, sociotechnical theory offers promise, especially in terms of "creating the conditions for cohesive, expert, flexible teams that relate well to a wider system" (Jenkins, Salmon, Stanton, & Walker, 2008, p. 495). Sena and Shani (1994) added that the social subsystem also includes relationships within groups and between groups.

Sociotechnical theory has evolved over time to adapt to organizations that are more technology and information systems based. For example,

Cherns (1976) developed nine general principles of sociotechnical design for use in designing work methods for manufacturing organizations. Clegg (2000) expanded Cherns's principles by developing a set of sociotechnical principles for systems design emphasizing that systems managers and developers may use the principles when appropriately supported by methods and tools to help with design choices. Because project teams are utilized in all stages of systems design and involve interdependent social and technical subsystems, one of the key principles is the idea that the practice of systems design is itself a sociotechnical system (Clegg, 2000).

Researchers have investigated the relationship between sociotechnical theory and software development. Guinan and Sawyer (1998) claimed that software development is, at least in part, a social process, which means that project leaders must understand the process of how people work together to build software in addition to the technological aspects. In a 2004 study, Kendra and Taplin developed a 2 x 2 model that depicted success factors on the micro and macro level for both social and technical dimensions:

1. The micro social dimension includes leadership behavior characteristics and the skills and competencies that project leaders need to manage projects.
2. The macro social dimension includes the organizational structures such as the cross-functional team participants, senior management, software developers, client, and project manager.
3. The micro technical dimension includes a performance measurement system to help monitor project performance, schedule, budget, requirements, and software quality.
4. The macro technical dimension includes the supporting management practices such as project management processes, prioritization, vendor management, and software development frameworks to manage the software development activities.

Kendra and Taplin's (2004) model is relevant to project success in modern systems development because the elements of each of the four dimensions are independent of each other; however, in sociotechnical systems, the dimensions are interdependent. The adoption of a systems design structure that recognizes both the social and the technical aspects enables interaction between the elements (Kendra & Taplin, 2004).

Current themes in sociotechnical theory research and information systems call for evaluating the technical suitability of an SDM as well as fitting the social characteristics of an organization and the development team itself (Bajec & Vavpotic, 2009). Another theme involved utilizing a sociotechnical approach to improving the systems development process (Patnayakuni & Ruppel, 2010). Patnayakuni and Ruppel (2010) noted that the information systems process is embedded in a social and technical subsystem; therefore, improvement is found through the application of sociotechnical work design principles and the utilization of formalized SDMs. One of the common themes in software development research involves global or collocated software development. Sociotechnical theory is especially relevant as software development is becoming more of a multicultural, multisite, and globally distributed endeavor (Mishra & Mishra, 2011).

Structuration Theory

Giddens (1984) introduced the concepts of systems, structure, and the duality of structure. Structure represents the rules and resources in social systems. Systems have structures and refer to the relations between people, or agents, organized in social practices (Giddens, 1984). The structuration of systems refers to the duality of agents and structures and how the activities of actors, who draw upon the rules and resources in their normal actions, assist in producing and reproducing systems by their interactions across time and space (Giddens, 1984).

Orlikowski (2000) furthered structuration theory by addressing the role of improvisation and emergence in the area of technology use to extend the structuration perspective. The result of Orlikowski's concepts is a practice lens focused on human action and recurrent engagement with technology that produces and reproduces emergent structures of technology, which is also known as technologies in practice. In practical terms, a technological artifact is an object or tool, whether it is used or not. Technologies in practice allow for examining users' social practices versus design intentions and the properties inherent within a particular technology (Orlikowski, 2000).

Adaptive Structuration Theory

DeSanctis and Poole (1994) created AST as an extension of Gidden's (1984) structuration theory. According to DeSanctis and Poole, AST provides a means or approach to study the role of IT in organizational change initiatives and achieves this by two methods: (a) the types of structures provided by advanced technologies and (b) the structures that emerge in human action as people interact with technology (p. 121). One of the strengths of AST is that it "expounds on the nature of social structures within advanced information technologies and the key interaction processes that figure in their use" (DeSanctis & Poole, 1994, p. 121). AST also views groups as systems with patterns of relationships and interactions among agents who are creating structures.

In addition to Gidden's theory of structuration, AST was created based on several other theoretical approaches, the most notable being sociotechnical systems theory (DeSanctis & Poole, 1994). Like sociotechnical theory, AST extends to both the structure of advanced technologies and the social interaction that occurs as technology is used. In practice, IT has the potential to alter social structures and be affected by the use, design, and implementation of these structures simultaneously (Cresswell, Gil-Garcia, Luna-Reyes, & Zhang, 2005).

According to Bostrom, Chin, and Gopal (1993), AST utilizes *appropriation*. Appropriation refers to "the manner in which structures are adapted by a group for its own use through a process called structuration wherein structures are continuously produced and reproduced" (Bostrom et al., 1993, p. 47). In an effort to apply the concepts of AST to systems support use for groups, Bostrom et al. maintained that AST, much like open-systems theory, utilizes an input–process–output framework. The input conditions would include items such as the technology, the task type, facilitation, group size, or group history. The process includes the groups creating and adapting structures, which is characterized by their appropriation. The output refers to the perceived quality, satisfaction with the outcome, or satisfaction with the process (Bostrom et al., 1993).

Loureiro-Koechlin (2008) noted that from a structuration standpoint, software development has two modes: a design mode and a use mode. The design mode refers to the human action and the use mode represents the technology that affects human action (Loureiro-Koechlin, 2008). AST has also been used as a theoretical foundation to study the adaption and appropriation of agile systems (Cao, Mohan, Ramesh, & Xu, 2009). According to Cao et al. (2009), "Agile methods provide structure through the rules and constraints they advocate. Project and task characteristics also impose structure on the development team" (p. 39). The relevance of these studies can be found in the relationship of software development as factors of both technology and human action, whereas the use of SDMs may be able to provide the structure needed for IT project success (Cao et al., 2009).

The Evolution of Leadership Theory

Leadership theories have evolved greatly over time. Many early-20th-century theorists believed that leadership was born in people and only persons with certain innate attributes or skills were capable of being leaders. This great man theory was quickly improved with trait theories, where leadership was explained in terms of traits of personality and character (Stogdill, 1974). Stogdill (1974) also maintained that social scientists developed newer theories to include the effects of certain situations on leadership (situational theory), the effects of behaviors and rewards (path-goal theory), and the effects of demands imposed by the situation (contingency theory).

According to Northouse (2004), the leader–member exchange theory (LMX) challenged previous assumptions that leadership was something performed on all followers. Rather, LMX theory proposed that differences may exist between a leader and each follower. Northouse noted that it is important for leaders to develop high-quality exchanges with all their subordinates rather than a select few.

Another theory that evolved was transformational theory. Burns (1978) was the first theorist to make a distinction between transactional and transformational theories. Transactional theory refers to most of the previous leadership models in that they tend to focus on exchanges between leaders and subordinates. Transformational theory was a newly emerging theory that included a focus on the connection between a leader and a follower and the leader's ability to inspire or influence followers so that the followers might reach their greatest potential (Northouse, 2004).

McGregor (2006) noted that when managers make decisions, they have certain assumptions regarding human nature and human behavior. The assumptions resulted in the creation of two opposing theories: Theory X and Theory Y. The basis of Theory X is the core assumptions that humans dislike work, avoiding it if possible, and that most workers have to be controlled, directed, or threatened to get the needed amount of effort. Conversely, the core assumptions for Theory Y include the belief that mental and physical effort is natural, workers' commitment to achieving their objectives is a function of rewards and recognition for achievement, most humans learn to accept and seek responsibility, and most humans have the ability to exercise imagination, ingenuity, and creativity to solve problems (McGregor, 2006).

McGregor (2006) contended that both theories may be used in one organization or even by one leader. However, McGregor challenged leaders to be open-minded and adopt more positive views of workers, which meant striving to operate under the tenets of Theory Y rather than Theory X. From a theoretical perspective, Theory Y is more conducive to IT settings where the organizational climate supports a need for leaders to be able to manage projects and allow software developers and other IT personnel to be creative. With the evolution of leadership theory and the ensuing and increasing complexity since the late 1940s, the focus of more current theories shifted in response to business and organizational shifts as well as conditions that changed rapidly with new levels of technology, diversity, and competition (McGregor, 2006).

Leadership Style

Leadership style is a concept that different theorists can define and categorize differently. According to Chemers (1997), the concept of leadership style fits "somewhere between the broad personality trait and the specific behavior" (p. 21), where the styles reflect "relatively stable patterns of response to stable situations" (p. 21). The earliest reference and research concerning leadership style is in the 1939 germinal work by Lewin, Lippit, and White, who examined authoritarian, democratic, and laissez-faire leadership styles and their effect in experimental situations with children. The findings supported the assertion that fewer displays of tension and aggression occurred under the democratic leadership style (Lewin et al., 1939).

Other researchers have performed studies using other classifications of leadership style, including charismatic, task oriented, and relationship oriented (Bowen-Thompson, DeCaro, & Decaro, 2010; Shore, 2005); democratic and autocratic (Nkenchor & Ottu, 2010); human-oriented, task-oriented, and charismatic (Bakker-Pieper & de Vries, 2009); and exploitive authoritative, benevolent authoritative, consultative, and participative (Rad & Yarmohammadian, 2006). One example of the use of transformational leadership and transactional leadership as leadership styles in research appeared in a study on personality characteristics and leadership styles of IT managers using agile methods (Bonner, 2010). Bonner (2010) contended agile development requires leadership styles that are suitable for organizational cultures that support adaptation and innovation rather than coercive tactics.

Another way to categorize leadership style is to view each component of the full range of transformational leadership model as a leadership style, including transformational leadership, transactional leadership, and laissez-faire leadership (Bodla & Nawaz, 2010). Bodla and Nawaz (2010) examined the relationship of each of the five factors or dimensions specifically associated with the transformational leadership style and satisfaction in a correlational study. The findings confirmed the hypothesis that each of the five factors, and thus transformational leadership style as a whole, had a positive, significant relationship with follower satisfaction (Bodla & Nawaz, 2010).

Even though the use of leadership styles in research has included many different methods of categorization, the current study included the concepts of the full range of transformational leadership model to assess leadership style. The next sections include an examination of the concepts of transformational leadership theory and the full range of transformational leadership model as well as how they were utilized in current research.

Transformational Leadership Theory

The first theorist to make a distinction between transactional and transformational leadership was Burns in 1978. Burns (1978) maintained that within a leader–follower relationship, an interaction occurs between people with different skills and motivations for a common purpose. Transactional leadership focuses on an exchange between the leader and the follower, whereas transformational leadership occurs when "one or more persons engage with others in such a way that leaders and followers raise one another to higher levels of motivation and morality" (Burns, 1978, p. 20). Burns believed that the interaction between leaders and followers can be either transactional or transformational in form.

Bass and Riggio (2006) purported that instead of being two separate theories as Burns suggested, transformational leadership is an extension of transactional leadership. While agreeing that transactional leadership emphasizes an exchange between the leader and the follower, Bass and Riggio maintained that transformational leaders rise to the next level by helping followers to develop into leaders themselves through "responding to individual follower's needs by empowering them and aligning the objectives and goals of the individual followers, the leader, the group, and the larger organization" (p. 20). According to Bass and Riggio, effective leadership may require both transactional and transformational attributes.

One of the tenets of TL theory is that leadership is a process that occurs between two parties: a leader and a follower (Northouse, 2004). Burns (1978) contended that the transformational leader takes the initiative in the leader–follower relationship by creating links that allow exchange and communication. Leaders also take the major role of maintaining the relationship with followers and "ultimately carrying out the combined purpose of leaders and followers" (Burns, 1978, p. 20), which indicates that the responsibility of the leader–follower transformational relationship lies almost solely with the leader. However, later theorists dispute this (Northouse, 2004). In transformational leadership, "leadership is not the sole responsibility of a leader but rather emerges from the interplay between leaders and followers" (Northouse, 2004, p. 184). According to Bass and Riggio (2006), because the transformational leader individualizes the needs of the followers, it is actually a process that involves both parties' needs.

The Full Range of Transformational Leadership Model

Bass added to Burns's original ideology by maintaining that transformational leadership is an expansion of transactional leadership (Avolio & Bass, 1994). Based on this expansion theory, Avolio and Bass created the full range of leadership model that includes aspects of both transactional and transformational leadership. As seen in Figure 5, transformational leadership consists of four major components: idealized influence (attributes and behaviors), inspirational motivation, intellectual stimulation, and individualized consideration. The four components from transformational leadership are included, as are two components of transactional leadership: contingent reward and management-by-exception (active or passive). The final piece in the model is laissez-faire leadership (Avolio & Bass, 1994; Bass & Riggio, 2006).

Leadership Style	Attributes	MLQ-5X Components
Transformational Leadership	Leaders' behavior allows them to serve as a role model. Leaders are admired, respected, and trusted. Leaders also demonstrate high standards, persistence, and determination.	Idealized influence
	Leaders will instill pride in others and will go beyond self-interest for the good of the group. The leader will act in ways that will build respect and display confidence.	Idealized attributes
	Leaders will discuss important values and beliefs, will have a strong sense of purpose, and will consider moral and ethical consequences. Collective sense of mission.	Idealized behaviors
	Leaders' behavior inspires and motivates by providing meaning and challenge. Display optimism and enthusiasm. Leaders clearly communicate expectations and vision.	Inspirational motivation
	Stimulate efforts to be innovative and creative. Creativity is encouraged. New ideas and approaches are solicited without criticism.	Intellectual stimulation
	Leaders act as a coach or mentor and pay attention to followers' need for achievement and growth. Interaction is personalized and individual differences accepted.	Individual consideration
Transactional Leadership	Leaders obtaining agreement from followers on tasks with promised rewards in exchange for satisfactory completion of assignment.	Contingent reward
	Leaders will actively monitor followers' work for mistakes, errors, or deviance from standards. Will take corrective action as necessary.	Management by exception
	Form of management by exception that is more passive and reactive. Leaders do not respond to situations and problems systematically.	Passive avoidant behavior
	Leaders passively wait for followers to make mistakes, errors, or deviate from standard. Only then will the leader take corrective action.	Management by exception (passive)
Laissez-Faire Leadership	Avoidance or absence of leadership. Leader will avoid getting involved, decisions are not made, actions are delayed, and leadership responsibility is ignored.	Laissez-faire

Figure 5. The components of the full range of transformational leadership model.

According to Avolio and Bass (2004), the MLQ 5X was developed based on the constructs of the full range of leadership model to create a new paradigm and to understand the higher and lower order effects of leadership. The new paradigm of transactional and transformational leadership was built upon earlier leadership paradigms such as the directive versus participative leadership style or the autocratic versus democratic leadership style (Avolio

& Bass, 2004). Avolio and Bass also purported that both transactional leadership and transformational leadership could be either participative or directive.

Avolio and Bass (2004) have revised and improved the MLQ 5X over time, but the most current edition includes 45 items. Nine of the 45 items measure outcomes, including "ratings of the leader's effectiveness, satisfaction with the leader, and the extent to which followers exert extra effort as a result of the leader's performance" (Avolio & Bass, 2004, p. 21). The other 36 standardized items include each of the nine leadership dimensions assessed by four items each. According to Bass and Avolio (2006), in terms of reliability, the alpha coefficient for the MLQ across scales is .80. The rate–rerate consistency scores for follower ratings ranged between .52 and .82 (Bass & Riggio, 2006). Avolio and Bass (2004) maintained that the construct validity for the MLQ has been analyzed, and the latest instrument (5X) was improved over the previous version (5R) using confirmatory factor analysis. In addition, multiple researchers have examined the performance of the MLQ, and the instrument is the best practiced measurement for analyzing leadership (Avolio & Bass, 2004).

Research Involving Transformational Leadership

According to Northouse (2004), more than 200 theses, dissertations, and research projects have been conducted on the topic of transformational leadership. Lowe and Gardner (as cited in Northouse, 2004, p. 184) found from their content analysis that 34% of the leadership articles in *Leadership Quarterly* were on the topic of transformational and charismatic leadership. Although much research has been conducted in the area of transformational leadership in general and across many subject areas, very little research is specific to IT personnel and software development. Some relevant research included an examination into transformational leadership and its link to individual performance, innovation, and leading project teams.

Individual performance. Although transformational leadership is generally accepted as a popular approach by effective leaders in organizations, much research is geared toward the mechanisms that more fully explain the influences of transformational leadership. According to Bass and Riggio (2006), a transformational leader will motivate and inspire followers to transcend their own needs in an effort to gain their commitment toward the vision and goals of the organization. In essence, the leader will motive the follower to higher levels of performance.

One line of inquiry in this area is that high levels of performance include the existence of organizational citizenship behaviors (OCBs). OCBs include characteristics such as courtesy, peacemaking, spreading goodwill, conscientiousness, job dedication, helping coworkers, enthusiasm, and extra effort (Bono et al., 2006). According to Colquitt and Piccolo (2006), transformational leaders are able to raise task performance and encourage OCBs through followers' perceptions of their core job characteristics. For example, leaders can enhance the followers' perceptions of variety and autonomy in their jobs by seeking new perspectives or by developing new ways for the followers to perform their job tasks (Colquitt & Piccolo, 2006). Hackman and Oldham (1975) identified autonomy as one of the five characteristics of jobs that affect motivation, performance, and satisfaction. These concepts support the link between transformational leadership and OCB. However, Bono et al. (2006) also maintained that an important link exists between OCB and job satisfaction.

The link between transformational leadership and job satisfaction appears in other studies as well. For example, in two studies designed to examine the relationship of transformational leadership and work outcomes in the China, India, Kenya, and the U.S. banking sector, Lawler, Shi, Walumbwa, and Wang (2004) and Lawler and Walumbwa (2003) found that self- and collective efficacy have a moderating effect between transformational leadership and work outcomes such as job satisfaction and organizational commitment. Additionally, a study designed to examine intrinsic and extrinsic factors, job satisfaction, and transformational leadership behaviors revealed that employees' personality traits, job characteristics, and managers' transformational leadership styles all related to high job satisfaction (Ho, Kuo, Lin, & Wu, 2010).

Innovation and project team success. Support for innovation exists within the intellectual stimulation component of transformational leadership. Transformational leaders stimulate followers and their efforts to be creative or innovative by soliciting new ideas, encouraging new approaches to old situations or problems, and reframing problems (Avolio & Bass, 1994; Bass & Riggio, 2006). In a study designed to examine transformational leadership, creativity, and innovation in software development companies, the findings supported the assertions that a positive association exists between transformational leadership and employee creativity (Gumusluoglu & Ilsev, 2009). According to Gumusluoglu and Ilsev (2009), transformational leadership is positively related to organizational innovation as well. These concepts also support the idea that an appropriate leadership style is needed to stimulate creativity, which also supports Amabile's (1997) assertion that creativity is important for employees in software development and other high-technology fields.

Lemons, Nath, and Parzinger (2001) designed a study to examine the effects of transformational leadership style compared to transactional leadership style utilized during a total quality management implementation in the area of software development. A significant positive increase occurred in total quality management program success when the leader's style was predominantly transformational rather than transactional (Lemons et al., 2001). In practical terms, leaders had more success by offering support and motivation than those who strictly defined expectations and reward employees based solely on the accomplishment of goals.

Other researchers have looked for variables that explain how and when TL influences team innovation. For example, Boener, Eisenbeiss, and Kippenberg (2008) contended that the effect of transformational leadership on team innovation is enabled within the factors of team climate. Specifically, the factors of team climate include support for innovation and climate for excellence. Thus, Boener et al. theorized that transformational leadership influences team innovation through support for innovation, but only under high levels of climate for excellence. In practical terms, Boener et al.'s research supported the idea that in organizational settings where innovation is required to remain competitive, transformational leaders should strive to provide clear performance criteria, promote high-quality standards, and elicit team members' commitment to the team and organizational goals (Boener et al., 2008).

Another researcher who examined a link between transformational leadership and project team performance was Keller (2006), who examined research and development teams. Keller theorized that within teams, leaders can intellectually stimulate members to consider alternative ways of approaching problems and provide an appropriate initiating team structure of roles and activities to attain team goals. The results indicated that transformational leadership positively affected project team leadership, but more specifically, the intellectual stimulation component of transformational leadership and initiating structure positively predicted project team performance (Keller, 2006). Another study designed to examine 47 groups at four Korean firms showed that transformational leadership was positively related to empowerment, group cohesiveness, and group effectiveness (Jung & Sosik, 2002).

In looking at leadership style in general and the components of the full model of transformational leadership as leadership styles, it is evident that the research spans many different subject areas. The link between transformational leadership and individual follower performance and job satisfaction has been reported, as well as the link between transformational leadership and innovation and project team success (Bass & Riggio, 2006). In addition, the tenets of transformational leadership are supported by the concepts of sociotechnical theory and the idea that IT project leadership is more likely to be successful if the leader understands the need to manage both the human aspect as well as the technological process involved in software development.

Motivation

In examining the differing concepts of job satisfaction, motivation theories have provided insight into human behavior and understanding what drives employee attitudes and behavior in the workplace. Understanding motivation theory also informs the understanding of how technical and social subsystems can affect employee attitudes, behavior, and job satisfaction. Much of the research in the area of motivation is instrumental in helping managers understand how to influence the desired outcomes for the betterment of employees and the organization as well.

Maslow's Hierarchy of Needs Theory

Maslow's hierarchy of needs is one of the original humanistic theories in motivation. Maslow (1943) maintained that employees are motivated not by organizational demands or tactics but by their own physiological and psychological needs. Most of the needs are depicted in a triangular model whereby the most simplistic and basic needs are on the bottom and the highest, most complex needs are on the top.

Maslow (1943) asserted that there are five levels of needs that start with one's physiological needs for food, water, warmth, and sleep. These basic physiological needs must be met to address the next set of needs. The next level is safety, which provides for one's needs for safety and security. As employees progress up the ladder, their basic physiological needs are being met and they are moving toward meeting their psychological and social needs (Maslow, 1943).

After employees have met their need for security and safety, the next step is to meet their need for belonging, love, friendship, and intimacy. This level illuminates the need for leaders to recognize social subsystems and realize the importance of fostering conditions that allow employees to collaborate with other team members and to interact in a social context (Cherry & Robillard, 2008). This level is the last in Maslow's (1943) hierarchy that is considered a base need.

The fourth level in Maslow's (1943) hierarchy is esteem, which refers to one's need for self-worth, recognition, and accomplishment. In an organizational IT setting, esteem or self-worth is increased by recognition of one's accomplishments and performance achievements, which gives employees a sense that they have contributed to the organization's success (Maslow, 1998). Many studies have been conducted over the past few decades to examine which factors motivate and demotivate IT personnel (Baddoo, Beecham, Hall, Robinson, & Sharp, 2008a, 2008b; Baddoo & Hall, 2002). Some of the motivating factors in these studies for software developers include recognition for a high-quality job performed based on objective criteria, benefits and pay linked to performance, and the possibility of advancement (Baddoo et al., 2008a). All these factors relate to the fourth level in Maslow's (1943) hierarchy, as they are all related to recognition, accomplishment, and ultimately to one's self-esteem.

The fifth level on Maslow's (1943) hierarchy is self-actualization. This level is the hardest to achieve for employees or people in general, as it involves reaching a level of self-fulfillment or one's highest potential. According to Maslow (1943), a person can reach the top level only when all the other needs have been met, and because most people tend to focus on their basic needs, they may never reach self-actualization.

Maslow's (1943) hierarchy of needs, particularly the fourth and fifth levels, is especially relevant for IT leaders and IT personnel. In L. Chen's 2007 study designed to examine the relationship between achievement motivation, job characteristics, and job satisfaction for IT personnel, the findings supported L. Chen's assertion that feedback, professionalism, and autonomy will affect job satisfaction. IT leaders should understand the link between employees' motivators and job satisfaction because "the main reason why IS personnel wish to perform jobs with high feedback and professionalism is because they hope to achieve self-actualization and social satisfaction" (L. Chen, 2007, p. 114). L. Chen's study and assertions supported the fourth and fifth level of Maslow's hierarchy of needs.

According to the principles of sociotechnical theory, in addition to being able to manage the technical aspects of an IT project, IT leaders must also be able to manage the human aspects (Clegg, 2000). The factors that motivate IT personnel lead to job satisfaction and are ultimately linked to voluntary turnover, such as creativity, autonomy, collaboration, and receiving feedback, are factors that IT leaders must manage throughout the software development process (Amabile, 1997; Aurum & Ghapanchi, 2011; Colquitt & Piccolo, 2006). In a study designed to examine group creativity, job satisfaction, and turnover intention, Fleischman, Godkin, Kidwell, and Valentine (2011) found that group creativity was positively related to job satisfaction, and job satisfaction was clearly negatively linked to turnover intention.

Herzberg's Motivation-Hygiene Theory

Herzberg's (1987) motivation-hygiene theory is another of the original contributions to the study of motivation. Herzberg created a two-component model that included items that influence people. The first component includes items that can lead to job dissatisfaction and are called *hygiene factors*. According to Herzberg, hygiene factors such as pay, benefits, supervision, status, job security, and working conditions are important, but their presence is not a motivator. In fact, the absence of these factors will lead to job dissatisfaction. For example, having decent working conditions is not a motivator and is not linked to job satisfaction, but bad working conditions will lead to job dissatisfaction (Herzberg, 1987).

The second component in Herzberg's (1987) motivation-hygiene theory includes motivators or growth factors. These factors give positive satisfaction such as achievement, recognition, the work itself, responsibility, growth, and promotion. The motivator factors come from intrinsic conditions of the job rather than hygiene factors, which are extrinsic to the job itself (Herzberg, 1987).

Many of Herzberg's ideas of motivation are similar to Maslow's perspectives on self-actualization. Herzberg (1987) asserted that if leaders can devote their efforts toward job enrichment, "the return in human satisfaction and economic gain would be one of the largest dividends that industry and society have ever reaped through their efforts" (p. 117). Herzberg believed that by allowing employees to take more control and responsibility in their jobs, employees could reach a higher level of job enrichment.

Both Maslow (1943) and Herzberg (1987) shared the idea that workers can reach self-actualization or high levels of job enrichment, which is the means by which job satisfaction may be achieved. Some differences exist between the two theories as well. Maslow's hierarchy of needs starts with an individual's most basic physiological needs and from there he or she can achieve meet psychological needs. Herzberg believed that base needs such as hunger are related to people's animal nature rather than human nature. Herzberg created this model based on human nature motivators and thus did not specify whether physiological or psychological needs were more important. Rather, Herzberg believed that both must be satisfied to be motivated. Based on Maslow's theory, offering an employee a raise is a motivator because it meets base needs as well as a sense of achievement. In contrast, Herzberg believed that receiving more pay is a hygiene factor and increasing wages only motivates employees to seek the next pay increase.

In terms of IT personnel and job satisfaction, like Maslow's (1943) hierarchy of needs, Herzberg's (1987) motivation-hygiene theory highlights the need for IT leaders to be cognizant of the factors that motivate their employees and affect job satisfaction. Factors such as pay and benefits are not considered motivators; however, factors such as achievement, recognition, the work itself, responsibility, and growth are motivators related to job enrichment. Herzberg contended that job enrichment provides an opportunity for employees' psychological growth and is ultimately related to job satisfaction. Many studies designed to examine motivation and job satisfaction for IT personnel have supported Herzberg's assertions (Baddoo et al., 2008a, 2008b; Baddoo & Hall, 2002).

Hackman and Oldham's Job Characteristics Model

Although Herzberg's (1987) motivation-hygiene theory hinted of designing, or redesigning, work based on factors that motivate employees, it was Hackman and Oldham (1975) who further developed concepts around redesigning work. Hackman and Oldham identified five characteristics of jobs that affect motivation, performance, and satisfaction (p. 395):

1. Skill variety: The degree to which a job requires the use of different skills and talents.
2. Task identity: The degree to which a job requires completion in whole and with a recognizable outcome.
3. Task significance: The degree to which a job has a substantial effect, either to the organization or to external customers.

4. Autonomy: The degree to which a job allows freedom, independence, and discretion to the worker.

5. Feedback: The degree to which completing activities results in clear and direct information about the employee's performance.

Hackman and Oldham (1975) also developed an instrument called the Job Diagnostic Survey to measure the following: (a) objective job characteristics, or the degree to which jobs are designed so that they enhance work motivation and job satisfaction, (b) reactions of employees to their jobs and work setting, and (c) the readiness of individuals for jobs with high potential for generating internal work motivation. Based on Hackman and Oldham's (1975) theory of how jobs affect employee motivation, the Job Diagnostic Survey is intended to diagnose existing jobs to determine if redesigning them could improve employee productivity and satisfaction.

Hackman and Oldham's (1975) model can be used for different types of work and different types of organizations. As the environment for IT and technology changes can include a fast pace, IT personnel have to be able to adapt to new tasks and roles. Researchers have used the job characteristics model in numerous studies that involve the technology field. For example, Griesser (1993) examined information systems developers and maintenance personnel and their growth needs, technology strength, and change acceptance. The findings indicated that IT developers benefit more from these variables and will respond more positively when given the opportunity to stretch their abilities, which will offer higher personal growth (Griesser, 1993). Ho et al. (2010) designed a study to examine the effect of work redesign for IT professions. The results confirmed that a positive relationship exists between work redesign on empowerment and organizational commitment (Ho et al., 2010). Empowerment and the opportunity to stretch one's abilities are tied to creativity, which is important for software development and other high-technology fields (Amabile, 1997).

Motivation in IT

In looking at motivation relevant to technical jobs and IT personnel, Amabile (1997) examined how to motivate creativity in organizations. Theorists have typically viewed intrinsic and extrinsic motivators as completely separate, where the introduction of one may hinder the other. Amabile asserted that "certain forms of extrinsic motivation may combine synergistically with intrinsic motivations" (p. 45). The three factors involved are the initial level of intrinsic motivation, the type of extrinsic motivation, and the timing of extrinsic motivation.

Amabile (1997) developed the intrinsic motivation principle of creativity. According to Amabile, "Intrinsic motivation is conducive to creativity. Controlling extrinsic motivation is detrimental to creativity, but informational or enabling extrinsic motivation can be conducive, particularly if initial levels of intrinsic motivation are high" (p. 46). If the conditions are right, extrinsic and intrinsic motivators can work together to create an environment that is conducive to high creativity, which is important in high-technology fields where developers or engineers must visualize innovative solutions.

The importance of the intrinsic motivation principle of creativity was described in the study conducted by Amabile (1997) involving a high-technology company where several factors were shown to be positively related to creative work outcomes. The factors were freedom, positive challenge, work group support, supervisory encouragement, organizational encouragement, and adequate resources. The findings of the study supported Amabile's assertions that (a) all work should be matched to people so that their skilled are matched, stretched, and valued by the company; (b) organizations should stress innovation throughout; and (c) work groups should be comprised of individuals with diverse skills and led by leaders who incorporate clearly set goals, appropriate autonomy, and performance feedback. In practical terms, Amabile's study supported the idea that motivation is more complex than originally considered in the theories of Maslow and Herzberg and that motivating for creativity in organizations, especially high-technology industries, is vital.

In support of Amabile's (1997) work, Bjorklund (2010) theorized that autonomy and goal clarity influence innovativeness, which affects IT personnel's motivation and initiative. Bjorklund further maintained that motivation and initiative are factors that ultimately support creativity. The study findings indicated that success factors supporting creativity in development projects include motivation, goal clarity, and autonomy and ultimately indicate the need for leaders to recognize and manage these factors in IT projects (Bjorklund, 2010).

Previous studies have indicated that motivators for software developers and other high-technology IT personnel may be different from other groups (Baddoo & Hall, 2002; Couger & Zawacki, 1980). Some motivational themes include the need for job autonomy, adequate resources, bottom-up initiatives, top-down organizational support, and process ownership (Baddoo & Hall, 2002). According to a meta-analysis performed by Baddoo et al. (2008b), one of the most frequently found motivators in the literature was the software developer's ability to identify with a task, which includes having clear goals, knowing the purpose of the task, understanding how the task fits in with the whole, and possessing the ability to create a quality product. Other common motivators from this study include the ability to use one's skills and be stretched, which is consistent with Amabile's (1997) ideology, as well as good management practices such as senior management support, good communication, and team building.

According to Whitaker (1997), having clear roles and responsibilities is a strong motivator for software developers. Whitaker's assertions supported the need for effective SDMs. Whitaker noted, "A software-development team always executes better when it uses a process—as long as everyone is accountable and everyone understands each milestone requirement" (p. 126). Whitaker also maintained that leaders who have an appropriate SDM and run the project correctly will be a motivator to the software developers and not a threat to their creativity.

Regarding IT industries, it is commonly thought that if leaders can improve how they manage software developers and better understand their motivators, companies can improve the ability to provide good quality software and information systems (Baddoo et al., 2008b). In addition to the ability to create a quality product, motivating software developers has been linked to increasing their job satisfaction and thereby reducing voluntary turnover (Lambert et al., 2001). Since the theories of Maslow and Herzberg came into fruition, researchers have conducted considerable research to have a better understanding of how to motivate employees and numerous studies have involved the area of IT personnel (Baddoo et al., 2008b).

Job Satisfaction

Even though motivation is not the same concept as job satisfaction, the two are clearly linked. The definition of job satisfaction can vary from theorist to theorist as well. Spector (1997) maintained that job satisfaction was merely how people feel about their jobs and differing aspects of their jobs. Other theorists have contended that job satisfaction is an emotional state based on how an individual appraises his or her job (Bono, Judge, & Locke, 2000), an affective reaction to one's job (Brief & Weiss, 2002), or just an attitude toward one's job (Brief, 1998).

Earlier Theories

According to Brief and Weiss (2002), many of the early studies regarding job satisfaction started in the 1930s and much of the ideology was based on the effect of work on employees. In 1976, Locke developed an important theory of the time: the range of affect theory. Locke believed that one's level of job satisfaction is more highly affected when a specific aspect of the job is important to the worker. In other words, job satisfaction is determined by what a person has in a job compared to what he or she desires in a job. Locke's theory has been used in many different studies to examine the relationship between the worker and expectations for jobs. For example, Brief and Weiss (2002) designed a study to examine the relationship between job characteristics, core self-evaluation, and job satisfaction and revealed a strong relationship exists between core-self-evaluation and job satisfaction and that job complexity, or the actual attainment of challenging jobs, is a key variable in that relationship (Brief & Weiss, 2002).

About 10 years after Locke developed the range of affect theory, Near and Organ (1985) examined the cognitive effects on job satisfaction. In looking at the current theories and measures of job satisfaction, there was some argument over whether the well-used instruments of the day defined job satisfaction in affective terms and actually measured job satisfaction in cognitive terms (Near & Organ, 1985). The introduction of the theory of cognitive effects on job satisfaction caused many theorists to evaluate whether their previous measures were cognitive based, affective based, or both (Brief & Weiss, 2002).

Dispositional theory surfaced in the 1980s and indicated that the specific job does not really matter because people have innate dispositions to be satisfied or not regardless of the work they do (Judge & Larson, 2001). Based on existing ideas of dispositional theory, Durham, Judge, Kluger, and Locke (1998) developed a core self-evaluations model that indicated certain core dispositional characteristics such as self-esteem, self-efficacy, locus of control, and neuroticism would all directly relate to job satisfaction and life satisfaction (Durham et al., 1998; Durham, Judge, & Locke, 1997).

Many models are considered contributory in areas of both motivation theory and job satisfaction. For example, the motivation-hygiene theory was one of the original contributions to motivation theory, but Herzberg (1987) also maintained that job satisfaction is driven by the motivational factors and job dissatisfaction is driven by hygiene factors. Another example is Hackman and Oldham's (1975) job characteristics model that identifies the characteristics of jobs that affect not only motivation but job satisfaction as well.

Spector's Job Satisfaction Survey

Spector's (1985) theories on job satisfaction were based on the belief that most of the previous studies, and consequently any generalizations, came primarily from industrial organizations. Spector created the JSS in an effort to meet the need for an instrument that could be used effectively in the area of human services. The development of the JSS was based on the theoretical position that job satisfaction is an affective or attitudinal reaction rather than cognitive or dispositional (Spector, 1985).

Based on research from the literature, Spector (1985) identified nine items or dimensions that would "adequately sample the domain of job satisfaction so that a combined score (sum of all subscales) would yield a good measure of overall satisfaction" (p. 699). According to Spector, the nine items are pay, promotional opportunities, contingent awards (appreciation and recognition), fringe benefits, coworkers, supervision, communication, the nature of the work itself, and work conditions. Each of the nine facets has four items on the instrument, some worded positively and some negatively, for a total of 36 items. There is also an overall total satisfaction score for a total of 10 possible scores (Spector, 1997).

Based on information gathered from 19 different samples collected, Spector (1985) performed various tests such as internal consistency validity (coefficient alpha), test–retest reliability, discriminant validity, and convergent validity. All tests indicated that the JSS exceeded the minimum requirements for validity, internal consistency, and reliability. The results of the factor analysis and other tests performed indicated that employees were able to have varying attitudes about differing aspects of their jobs, which provided strong evidence for the multidimensionality of job satisfaction (Spector, 1985).

Other Job Satisfaction Instruments

In addition to Spector's JSS (1985) and Hackman and Oldham's (1975) Job Diagnostic Survey, other instruments have been developed. The Job Descriptive Index (Hulin, Kendall, & Smith, 1969) includes the five facets of work, pay, promotion, supervision, and coworkers. Unlike most instruments that use a Likert-type scale, the JDS uses a short phrase that is descriptive of the job and responses include yes, no, or uncertain (Hulin et al., 1969).

The Minnesota Satisfaction Questionnaire (MSQ; Dawis, England, Lofquist, & Weiss, 1967) includes 20 different facets and has two forms, the 100-item version and the 20-item version. The 20 facets of the MSQ are activity, independence, variety, social status, supervision (human relations), supervision (technical), moral values, security, social service, authority, ability utilization, company policies, compensation, advancement, responsibility, creativity, working conditions, coworkers, recognition, and achievement (Dawis et al., 1967). Some of the facets of the MSQ are more specific than for the JSS; however, Spector (1997) noted that in some cases, a facet of the JSS is reflected in several of the MSQ facets. One of the concerns of the MSQ is that some of the facets are highly intercorrelated, which suggests "that they may be assessing the same (or highly related) aspects of the job" (Spector, 1997, p. 16).

Job Satisfaction Research in IT

Much of the literature in the IT area falls under two themes that are closely related. Most research includes either the examination of factors that affect job satisfaction or factors of job satisfaction that affect turnover intention. Understanding the relationship between job satisfaction and software project success is critical to help IT managers take the appropriate actions to enhance job satisfaction, which affects project success and will help ensure critical business success factors are met (Eedara & Korrapati, 2010).

Turnover intention. When software developers leave their jobs, they take their knowledge with them. Retaining IT personnel and their knowledge is critical for maintaining an organization's competitive advantage (Hannon & Westlund, 2008). Aurum and Ghapanchi (2011) performed an extensive, systematic review of literature from 1980 through 2008 regarding the antecedents of IT personnel's intention to leave their jobs. The review provided five broad categories: individual, organizational, job-related, psychological, and environmental factors. Each of these factors includes three or four subcategories, and each subcategory has several items to consider. The results of the review indicated that the most common triggers of turnover intention include role ambiguity, role conflicts, organizational tenure, and low job autonomy (Aurum & Ghapanchi, 2011). Role ambiguity occurs when individuals have a lack of understanding concerning their role or are unclear about managerial expectations of their performance (Kahn, Quinn, Rosenthal, Snoek, & Quinn, 1964). Role conflict is the degree to which an employee's understanding of his or her job role differs from employer expectations (J. Collins & Tubre, 2000). The results of Aurum and

Ghapanchi's study are promising because role ambiguity, role conflict, and job autonomy are all factors that an IT project leader can manage.

Using Spector's nine facets of job satisfaction to study turnover intentions, Hannon and Westlund (2008) found a significant predicting relationship exists between all nine facets and software developers' turnover intentions. According to Calisir, Gumussoy, and Iskin (2009), organizational commitment and job satisfaction are both related to intention to quit, and organizational commitment is explained by job satisfaction and stressors such as role ambiguity, role conflict workload, and work–family conflict. The results of the study supported Calisir et al.'s assertions indicating that stressors have a strong relationship with job satisfaction, which has a strong relationship with voluntary turnover.

Other studies have examined the additional variable of project leadership and its effect on satisfaction and turnover intentions. Westlund (2007) performed a study to examine the retention of IT talent and the relationship of project leadership styles, job satisfaction, and turnover retention. The findings indicated that greater overall job satisfaction is related to lower turnover intentions, and high turnover is associated with lower satisfaction with supervisors. In addition, proactive project leaders tended to have more satisfied IT team members, and reactive project leaders were associated with less satisfaction in IT team members (Westlund, 2007).

Job satisfaction. In looking at the literature specific to the theme of factors that affect job satisfaction among IT personnel, the variables varied. One example includes the influence of creativity on software developers and their attitudes of innovation, which Gallivan (2003) theorized were related to job satisfaction. Gallivan's findings indicated that innovators, rather than adapters, have higher levels of job satisfaction (Gallivan, 2003). In another study, Sanchez (2010) found work environment had a strong relationship with job satisfaction for IT professional employees.

In many cases, job satisfaction is used in conjunction with other variables. For example, Ozer (2008) examined LMX relationships and their relationship to job satisfaction. The findings indicated that the LMX–job satisfaction relationship was stronger when there were higher levels of task autonomy for software developers (Ozer, 2008). In a similar study designed to examine the multidimensionality of LMX and its relationship to employee outcomes such as job satisfaction, commitment, and OCB, Ansari, Bhal, and Gulati (2008) found multiple mediators applied. The most relevant finding involved the dimension of LMX called LMX-affect, which includes informal interactions. Affective relationships with the leader result in employees having affective reactions to the job (job satisfaction), which leads to higher organizational commitment (Ansari et al., 2009).

Other research closely related to IT personnel and job satisfaction includes the relationship between individual job satisfaction and group task satisfaction (Griffin & Mason, 2002, 2003), the effects of gender on job satisfaction (Ghazawi, 2010), and the effects of tasks, salaries, and external influences on job satisfaction for IT employees in a comparison of former and current jobs (Niederman & Sumner, 2004). In spite of the wide array of studies that examine the relationship of factors of IT personnel and job satisfaction, very little research has been conducted in the area of SDMs and job satisfaction. One notable exception is a 2007 study conducted by Maurer and Tessem, who maintained that the use of SDMs, specifically agile methods, leads to higher motivation and job satisfaction. Many researchers have found factors such as autonomy, variety, significance, and feedback relate to job satisfaction; however, Maurer and Tessem theorized that the use of agile methods helps ensure that these factors are addressed in IT projects ultimately leading to job satisfaction for IT personnel. The findings from the study supported Maurer and Tessem's assertions, which also indicated support for utilizing SDMs in IT projects, especially agile methods.

Another study specific to job satisfaction and agile methods was a 2011 study conducted by Pedrycz, Russo, and Succi, who maintained that factors of agile methods, specifically pair programming, are related to job satisfaction. These factors examined in the study include communication, work sustainability, and work environment. The findings of the study by Pedrycz et al. indicated that these factors all positively relate to job satisfaction in IT personnel. Specifically, when used with pair programming, good communication between developers, having a sustainable amount of work, design changes that are communicated quickly, and having well-organized meetings are all factors that increase the probability of increasing job satisfaction (Pedrycz et al., 2011).

Relationship of the Study to Previous Research

As noted in chapter 1, the focus of the current study was SDM use in projects, the leadership style of IT project leaders, and IT personnel job satisfaction. Specifically, the first research question was designed to answer whether a relationship exists between SDM use and IT personnel job satisfaction. The second research question was designed to answer whether a relationship exists between the leadership style of IT project leaders who are SDM users versus nonusers and IT personnel job satisfaction. An examination of these variables required a review of current research on several factors, including the importance of SDM use, the factors of SDM acceptance in organizations, and the human versus technical aspects of leading IT projects. An exploration of leadership style and its link to IT projects and job satisfaction was required, as were motivators of IT personnel and factors of job satisfaction and turnover intention for IT personnel.

Theorists have approached SDM use from many different perspectives. Use of SDMs in IT projects is supported, indicating that SDMs provide consistency, quality-checked deliverables, and an engineering-like discipline to IT projects (Cray, 2009; Fields et al., 1998). Much of the research and discussion involve the technical aspects of an IT project while still indicating that SDMs involve process management as well as human management (Millet & Pinto, 1999). The importance of viewing software development projects from both a production and a social perspective cannot be understated (Guinan & Sawyer, 1998) and is supported by the tenets of sociotechnical theory (Bostrom & Heinen, 1977; Kendra & Taplin, 2004).

Research designed to examine specific SDMs supports the theory that software development is a highly complex activity with a high degree of variability characterized by the diversity of needed tools and the unpredictability of people involved in the process (Mahapatra et al., 2005). Theorists have noted that IT failures can be attributed to the methodology or lack of methodology (Aken, 2008), and current research supports the creation of agile methods as IT project leaders answer to the more complex issues faced by software developers (Avison & Fitzgerald, 2008). Newer agile methods are attributed to having a people orientation rather than most previous SDMs that tended to focus on the process alone (Avison & Fitzgerald, 2008).

Current literature indicated many factors are involved in the acceptance and use of SDMs, including those at the organizational level, leader level, and developer level. Researchers have used many theories to examine the adoption of SDMs, indicating that there is some reluctance by IT leaders and software developers to use SDMs (Livermore, 2008). However, the majority of the research supports the use of SDMs in IT projects.

The use of transformational and transactional leadership as leadership styles is supported in the literature, especially for agile software development and organizations that support adaption and innovation. Although little research exists regarding transformational leadership specific to software development, transformational leadership has been well researched, with many of the findings related to concepts of IT project management and IT personnel (Bass & Riggio, 2006). Much of the current literature included an examination of the relationship between transformational leadership and improved individual performance, innovation, employee creativity, and project team success (Boener et al., 2008; Keller, 2006). These factors are all important concepts for effective IT project management, where, in support of sociotechnical theory, leaders must understand both the technological aspects and how people work together to build software (Guinan & Sawyer, 1998).

In examining the current literature pertaining to motivation, many studies for IT personnel indicated that valid motivators are related to meeting IT personnel's need for self-worth, recognition, self-actualization (Maslow, 1943), and job enrichment (Herzberg, 1987). IT personnel may be motivated by engaging in a collaborative environment or having one's accomplishments recognized based on objective criteria, receiving feedback, autonomy, and creativity (Amabile, 1997; H. Chen, Jiang, Klein, & Liu, 2010; Cherry & Robillard, 2008), which also supports the theory that motivators for IT personnel in general are distinct from other groups of people (Baddoo & Hall, 2002; Couger & Zawacki, 1980). According to Baddoo et al. (2008b), in the study of motivators and IT software development, current research supports the idea that organizations can create quality products if IT leaders use their understanding of motivators effectively to improve how they manage their software development teams (Baddoo et al., 2008b).

Much of the literature in the area of IT personnel and job satisfaction is related to the study of factors that affect job satisfaction or lead to voluntary turnover. Current research indicates that some of the common triggers of voluntary turnover for IT personnel include role ambiguity or role conflict and low job autonomy (Calisir et al., 2009). The level of work environment, creativity, task autonomy, group task satisfaction, task significance, and in one particular study, the use of agile methods, are all factors related to IT personnel and job satisfaction (Amabile, 1997; Maurer & Tessem, 2007; Ozer, 2008; Sanchez, 2010).

Considering the historically low numbers of successful IT projects and the low percentage of IT projects that use SDMs, much of the research for SDM use includes their importance in software development, the factors of method adoption, or which method is more effective. These factors are all based on an underlying assumption that the value of SDM use is in its link to project success and user satisfaction. Consequently, in spite of support for SDM use in the literature, most of the research conducted to date was not based on whether SDM use has an effect on IT personnel and job satisfaction. In addition, much of the research for leadership style and transformational leadership can be linked to IT through individual performance, innovation, creativity, and team project success. However, there is little research on leadership style for IT project leaders specifically, regarding their use or nonuse of SDMs, including whether there is any existing relationship to IT personnel job satisfaction. The study of job satisfaction and voluntary turnover indicates there are important and somewhat unique factors to consider for IT personnel; however, to date there is little linkage to IT personnel in IT project teams, specifically those who use SDMs versus those who do not. The absence of empirical research in the literature regarding these factors indicates a formidable gap that requires further examination.

Conclusion

Empirical research has shown that the majority of studies in the area of SDMs involve IT project success, which SDM is more suited for IT projects, adaption issues in organizations, and user satisfaction. Clearly, little research has been conducted with regard to IT personnel and SDM use. This gap is further illustrated by empirical research in the area of leadership and leadership style that further emphasizes a call for the consideration and management of both technical and human subsystems in IT projects using sociotechnical theory. Motivation and job satisfaction present another dimension as both are influenced by human needs and values. Empirical studies show there is very little research specifically focusing on IT personnel's job satisfaction and SDM use. However, studies have illuminated the link between job satisfaction and factors of IT personnel such as autonomy, creativity, and feedback. Additionally, research has shown that factors such as role ambiguity, role conflict, and low job autonomy lead to higher turnover intention. Each of these factors is managed in IT projects. Although the failure rate of IT projects is high and their associated costs are high, the cost of turnover in IT personnel due to job dissatisfaction is also substantial, as is the subsequent potential knowledge attrition. The linkage between SDM use and job satisfaction for IT personnel has yet to be determined; therefore, the lack of existing research indicates a critical gap in the literature that requires further empirical, scholarly investigation.

Chapter 3 includes a detailed account of the methodology used in the current study. Chapter 4 contains a discussion on the data analysis techniques used to test the hypotheses and to answer the research questions. Chapter 5 includes an interpretation of the findings of the study, limitations, recommendations for action, recommendations for future research, and implications for social change.

Chapter 3: Research Method

The current quantitative, correlational study was designed to investigate the relationships between SDM use, leadership style, and job satisfaction. Chapter 3 includes a detailed explanation of the research questions, hypotheses, research design, data collection techniques, instrumentation, data analysis, and ethical protection of participants. The chapter also includes a justification for utilizing a correlational design to address the research questions and the methods used to support or reject the hypotheses. The research questions were as follows:

1. What is the relationship, if any, between formal SDM use and overall job satisfaction?
2. What is the relationship, if any, between leadership style of leaders who are SDM users versus leaders who are non-SDM users and overall job satisfaction?

Based on the research questions, the hypotheses were as follows:

$H1_0$: There is no relationship between formal SDM use and overall job satisfaction for IT software development team members.

$H1_a$: There is a relationship between formal SDM use and overall job satisfaction for IT software development team members.

$H2_0$: There is no difference in the relationship between leadership style of leaders who use SDM versus leaders who do not use SDM and overall job satisfaction for IT software development team members.

$H2_a$: There is a difference in the relationship between leadership style of leaders who use SDM versus leaders who do not use SDM and overall job satisfaction for IT software development team members.

Research Design

The current study was designed to utilize correlational methods to examine the relationships between SDM use, leadership style, and job satisfaction. Correlation analysis involves identifying potential associations between variables, and the measure of the linear relationship between two variables is considered the correlation between them (Miles & Shevlin,

2001). Correlation is rooted in a postpositive research paradigm based on the premise that "any perception of reality cannot be an objective picture but is drawn from empirical observation and existing theory" (Pickard, 2007, p. 10). According to Creswell (2009), a postpositivist paradigm is appropriate for studies with variables derived from hypotheses and research questions. Correlational methods were utilized for statistical data analysis to accept or reject the hypotheses and an electronic, Internet-based study was used for data collection. According to Creswell (2009), survey data collection methods target a sample of a population and study trends, attitudes, or opinions via a quantitative or numeric description.

Appropriateness of Design

Correlation was the most appropriate design for the study because its purpose is to examine the association between the variables, and according to Miles and Shevlin (2001), correlation is a measure of how linearly related two variables are. The type of inquiry in the study called for a quantitative research design to examine the relationship between independent variables SDM use and leadership style and the dependent variable job satisfaction. Correlation is a quantitative research design that does not require testing and retesting under experimental methods, nor does it require establishing cause and effect (Simon, 2006; Singleton & Straits, 2010).

The theory presented includes a supposition that the independent variables have an association with the dependent variable and consequently that examining this association will address the problem of the study, which was whether job satisfaction is influenced by the use of SDMs in IT projects. According to Simon (2006), to investigate a problem, an approach must be chosen that is the most suitable. Quantitative studies are associated with objectivity, statistics, and generalizability, whereas qualitative studies are most associated with reality, based on a perception that is "different for each person, changes over time, and derives meaning mainly from context"

(Simon, 2006, p. 37). These principles were primarily used to choose the most appropriate research design.

A qualitative case study design was considered for the study. According to Creswell (2009), case studies are bounded by time and activity, which means that researchers gather information by many different methods over a specific period. Case studies may involve the thorough exploration of programs, events, processes, or groups of individuals (Creswell, 2009). Further, Pickard (2007) asserted that case studies are appropriate when the research requires a holistic, in-depth approach from the perspective of all stakeholders. Although case studies are emergent in nature and "are not intended to produce generalizations, they are intended to allow for transferability of findings based on contextual applicability" (Pickard, 2007, p. 93). Because the current study was designed to determine the existence of relationships among variables and to generalize findings from a sample to a population rather than performing a descriptive or explanatory investigation, the use of a case study methodology was not appropriate.

A qualitative grounded theory design was also considered for the study. According to Creswell (2009), grounded theory involves multiple stages of data collection including the continual "comparison of the data with emerging categories and theoretical sampling of different groups to maximize the similarities and differences of information" (p. 13). Pickard (2007) indicated that grounded theory starts with open, broad questions and a focus on social processes or interactions. The researcher engaged in the research to determine what is happening and why it is happening. After the researcher started making observations and began the process of data collection, a focus began to emerge. Data analysis for grounded theory is inductive in nature and must occur throughout the process because it is crucial in the formulation of a theory grounded in the data. As more data are collected through empirical investigation, the theory develops, is refined, and is confirmed (Pickard, 2007). Grounded theory is appropriate when very little initial information exists, when there is a general question rather than specific research questions or hypotheses, and when the data collected need to be interpreted by the researcher for the purpose of discovery. Thus, the grounded theory method was not suitable for the study, where the purpose was to examine relationships between variables. The focus for grounded theory is discovering information in a systematic process that is not designed to answer specific research questions or test hypotheses.

A qualitative phenomenological approach was also considered for the study. According to Creswell (2009), phenomenology involves the practice of discovering what is common for all participants who have experienced a shared phenomenon. The researcher reduces the data from all the individual experiences of a specific phenomenon into a composite description of the universal essence of the experience (Creswell, 2007). The analysis for phenomenology avoids comparisons and identifying themes; rather, the purpose of the analysis is to examine an experience in detail and in depth so that the reader will have a better understanding of the phenomenon as an outsider who has never had the same experience (Pickard, 2007). Phenomenology is appropriate when the researcher has identified an item of human experience that is in need of further examination from a first-person point of view, including the underlying structure of the phenomenon (Creswell, 2007). Therefore, due to its specific focus on in-depth examinations of human experience, phenomenology was not an appropriate methodology for the study.

Qualitative methods allow for viewing the world in a holistic fashion where data may be collected in a natural fashion that is sensitive to the participants and their experiences (Creswell, 2007). Qualitative researchers tend to adopt an emergent design, engage multiple data sources, and utilize data analyses in an inductive process (Creswell, 2009). Quantitative methods tend to utilize the early creation of a theory that requires hypothesis testing (Creswell, 2009). According to Simon (2006), quantitative methods also tend to be objective, narrow, concise, and generalizable from a sample to a population. In addition, the data collected in a quantitative study tend to be structured in numbers or translatable into numbers (Simon, 2006).

Because qualitative data collection typically requires methods that are time consuming and in many cases involve observation by the researcher, the number of participants is usually small (Creswell, 2007). The target population of the study spanned multiple organizations that were geographically dispersed in the United States and potentially around the world. For a quantitative study requiring larger numbers of participants from geographically dispersed areas, an Internet survey is more cost effective and allows for easier data collection (Singleton & Straits, 2010). An Internet survey utilizing a Likert-type scale was created to collect information regarding SDM use, leadership style, and job satisfaction. The data collected were used to test the hypotheses created based on the research questions. According to Simon (2006), researchers use correlational research to "determine relationships between variables, and if a relationship exists, to determine a regression equation that could be used to make predictions about a population" (p. 43). Based on these criteria, the statistical analysis for the study included correlational methods to test the relationships between the independent and the dependent variables. Of all the research methods considered, a correlational design was most appropriate for the study.

Population

The population for the study consisted of actively employed persons working as members of a software development team. Participants included IT personnel involved in the creation of software programs including analysts, systems designers, software developers, quality assurance, database administrators, and systems administrators. Purposive sampling was used as the sampling technique because it allows participants to be chosen based on the researcher's expert judgment and ability to select participants who are representative of the population (Singleton & Straits, 2010). Singleton and

Straits (2010) also noted that the strategy for purposive sampling is to "identify important sources of variation in the population and then to select a sample that reflects this variation" (p. 174). The requirements for the population of the current study were that the participants have (a) worked on a software development team; (b) are at least 18 years of age; and (c) have at least 1 year of experience as an analyst, systems designer, software developer, quality assurance, database administrator, or systems administrator.

According to Singleton and Straits (2010), purposive sampling is a form of nonprobability case selection and is an acceptable alternative to probability sampling when random selection is not realistic. The basis for choosing purposive sampling was that a specific set of participants was required, and utilizing the researcher's expert judgment facilitated recruiting the members of the IT personnel community. Other sampling techniques, such as convenience sampling, random sampling, and stratified random sampling, were also considered, but were not appropriate for the study.

The study also utilized a snowball sampling technique. Snowball sampling is a referral sampling technique where the participants help find other participants with a specific range of skills that are not easily obtainable by other means (Singleton & Straits, 2010). Participants were asked to pass the survey link on to other colleagues who work on software development teams. The demographic questions were structured such that the participants' eligibility was ascertained at the beginning of the survey. The combination of a purposive and a snowball sampling strategy helped ensure that the survey is confined to a specific segment of the IT personnel community.

Sample

The sample of the study consisted of IT personnel who work as part of a software development team as an analyst, systems designer, software developer, software engineer, quality assurance, database administrator, or systems administrator. IT project leaders were not included. Participants were required to have been actively involved on a software development team of at least four persons and for an IT project having lasted at least 2 months within the past year. Due to the nature of the sampling technique, the participants could have been from any public, private, or federal organization of any size, in any industry, and from anywhere in the world.

The first step in the Internet survey distribution plan was to use purposive sampling to identify potential participants that match the criteria of being IT personnel who work on software development teams. The participant pool included friends, colleagues, and persons from e-groups and social and professional online network groups. After receiving Institutional Review Board (IRB) approval, number 06-22-11-0128057, the researcher disseminated the Internet survey to the identified pool of potential participants. Participants were informed of the purpose of the study and criteria for participation in the first section of the Internet survey. Upon completion of the Internet survey, as part of the snowball sampling strategy, participants were encouraged to forward the Internet survey link to any colleagues who were IT personnel and worked on software development teams.

According to Miles and Shevlin (2001), when considering correlation and regression as data analysis techniques, an increase in the sample size will cause a reduction in standard error, which will increase the chance of discovering a significant association. Having a small sample size may mean the researcher misses the detection of existing relationships between variables. The two main methods for determining a sample size include a simplified rule of thumb method and a power analysis (Miles & Shevlin, 2001). Miles and Shevlin noted that the rule of thumb method involves choosing a sample size based on recommendations or formulas provided by previous researchers; however, this use of sample size determination may produce misleading results in regression testing.

The more popular method of calculating sample size is power analysis. According to Miles and Shevlin (2001), power analysis calculation requires (a) the significance level or alpha, (b) the effect size, (c) the number of independent variables, and (d) the appropriate level of power. Because power analysis is so complex to calculate by hand (Miles & Shevlin, 2001), many researchers use software programs and calculators such as GPower 3.1.2 software (Buchner, Erdfelder, Faul, & Lang, 2007). According to Buchner et al. (2007), a priori power analysis provides an efficient method of determining sample size based on a set statistical power before the data collection occurs. Table 1 contains the factors used to determine the sample size for the study.

Table 1

Factors Used to Calculate the Minimum Sample Size

Factor	Parameters	Description
Alpha	.05	*p* value or Type 1 error
Predictors	2	Total number of predictors
Expected effect size	.15	For regression, effect sizes of .02, .15, and .35 are considered small, medium, and large, respectively.
Statistical power	.95	Should be greater than .80
Minimum sample size	89	

Ethical Consideration of Participants

The study was conducted in accordance with the guidelines set by the Walden University IRB, which were followed to ensure the ethical protection of the research participants. According to Simon (2006), voluntary participation ensures that the participants are not forced to participate or are "held captive to the study" (p. 65). Researchers must provide enough information about a study so prospective participants can make an informed decision about whether they want to participate (Singleton & Straits, 2010). Thus, the first section of the Internet survey explained the purpose of the study, how the information would be used and housed, how the participants' identities would remain confident, and the time needed to complete the survey (see Appendix B).

Additionally, participants filled out the survey confidentially and were assured that their responses would not be shared with their work organizations. A statement was included in the first section of the survey indicating that, by filling out the survey, the participants were granting consent. The first section of the survey included a statement requiring the participants to acknowledge that they had read and understood all the requirements of the study, including that they were free to quit the survey at any time. Only those who acknowledged the question with a *yes* received access to the survey. In addition, some preliminary questions were asked to ensure that participants have been involved in an IT software development team comprised of at least four members in the past year and had participated in a project of at least 2 months' duration. All the responses will remain in a password-protected database for 5 years and no paper copies will be created.

Instrumentation

An online survey instrument utilizing a cross-sectional design was used to collect data for the study. The use of online surveys allows for a cost- and time-efficient method of collecting data that is appriopriate for a quantitative correlation study (Singleton & Straits, 2010). The survey included three main topic areas: personal and team-based demographic data, leadership style, and job satisfaction. Personal demographic data included items such as age, gender, and years of experience. Team-based demographic data included collecting team information and the use of SDMs in their most recent IT project lasting at least 2 months. Analyzing the demographic data involved nominal and ratio measurement scales.

Leadership style data were collected via the MLQ 5X (Bass & Avolio, 1990). The job satisfaction data were collected via the JSS (Spector, 1997). Both the MLQ and the JSS utilize an interval measurement scale.

Demographic Factors

Personal and team-based demographic data were used to identify specific characteristics of the participants. Personal demographic questions included statistical analysis of factors such as gender, age, and years of experience. Regarding the participants' most recent IT project experience, the team demographic questions included whether the team used an SDM, the number of months spent on the software development team, the position on the team (i.e., analyst, developer), the number of members on the team, and the number of months the last IT software project took to complete. A complete list of demographic items are in Appendix C.

MLQ (5X)

Leadership style was measured by Bass and Avolio's MLQ 5X. Permission to use the instrument was granted (see Appendix D). According to Avolio and Bass (2004), the MLQ 5X was developed based on the constructs of the full range of leadership model to understand the higher and lower order effects of leadership. Avolio and Bass have revised and improved the MLQ 5X over time, but the most current edition includes 45 items. Nine of those items measure outcomes, including factors such as satisfaction with the participant's leader and ratings of the leader's effectiveness (Avolio & Bass, 2004). The other 36 standardized items include each of the nine leadership dimensions assessed by four items each. The current study included only the 36 standardized items.

According to Avolio and Bass (2004), the items of the MLQ 5X can be utilized in different ways for a total of eight different models. For example, the model *one leadership factor* utilizes one overall score from the

MLQ 5X that indicates the leader's overall leadership score or to what extent the leader exhibits leadership. The current study included the model *three correlated factors: transformational vs. transactional vs. passive-avoidant leadership* to measure these three factors as leadership styles. Regarding this three-factor model, Avolio and Bass noted,

> The first factor comprises all of the transformational components. The second general factor will be comprised of active transactional leadership in the form of contingent reward and active management-by-exception. Both of these transactional factors represent a clear delineation of agreements, expectations and enforcements. The third factor will consist of items that tap into leadership that is passive in correcting mistakes, or in the extreme, avoidant. (p. 49)

Each of the 36 survey items are linked with one of the three factors: transformational, transactional, or passive-avoidant leadership. Table 2 indicates these linkages.

Table 2

Multifactor Leadership Questionnaire Survey Items and Leadership Style Factors

Factor	Items
Transformational	2, 6, 8, 9, 10, 13, 14, 15, 18, 19, 21, 23, 25, 26, 29, 30, 31, 32, 34, 36
Transactional	1, 4, 11, 16, 22, 24, 27, 35
Passive-avoidant	3, 5, 7, 12, 17, 20, 28, 33

Validity and reliability. According to Avolio and Bass (2006), in terms of reliability, the alpha coefficient for the MLQ across scales is .80. The rate–rerate consistency scores for follower ratings ranged between .52 and .82 (Bass & Riggio, 2006). Avolio and Bass (2004) maintained that the construct validity for the MLQ has been analyzed and the latest instrument (MLQ 5X) was improved over the previous version (MLQ 5R) using confirmatory factor analysis. In addition, the performance of the MLQ has been examined by multiple researchers and is the best practice measurement for analyzing leadership (Avolio & Bass, 2004).

Sample MLQ 5X questions. Participants were asked to consider their IT project leader and rate 36 items based on a 5-factor Likert-type scale where 0 indicates *not at all* and 4 indicates *frequently, if not always*. The following five questions are samples of items from the MLQ 5X:

1. Talks enthusiastically about what needs to be accomplished.
2. Waits for things to go wrong before taking action.
3. Spends time teaching and coaching.
4. Avoids getting involved when important issues arise.
5. Discusses in specific terms who is responsible for achieving performance targets.

JSS

The JSS was used to measure overall job satisfaction. Permission to use the instrument was granted (see Appendix E). Created in 1985 for the human services, the JSS was updated in 1997 and has been used across many different areas of research (Spector, 1997). Based on research from the existing literature, nine items or dimensions were identified that would "adequately sample the domain of job satisfaction so that a combined score (sum of all subscales) would yield a good measure of overall satisfaction" (Spector, 1985, p. 699). The nine items were pay, promotional opportunities, contingent awards (appreciation and recognition), fringe benefits, coworkers, supervision, communication, the nature of the work itself, and work conditions (Spector, 1985). Each of the nine facets has four items on the instrument, some worded positively and some negatively, for a total of 36 items. The negative items require reverse scoring (Spector, 1994). The item numbers and their direction appear in Table 3. There is also an overall total satisfaction score for a total of 10 possible scores (Spector, 1997).

Table 3

Item Numbers and Direction from the Job Satisfaction Survey

Direction	Items
Positive	1, 3, 5, 7, 9, 11, 13, 15, 17, 20, 22, 25, 27, 28, 30, 33, 35
Negative	2, 4, 6, 8, 10, 12, 14, 16, 18, 19, 21, 23, 24, 26, 29, 31, 32, 34, 36

Validity and reliability. Based on information gathered from 19 different samples, Spector (1985) performed various tests such as internal consistency validity (coefficient alpha), test–retest reliability, discriminant validity, and convergent validity. All tests indicated that the JSS exceeded the minimum requirements for validity, internal consistency, and reliability. Based on a sample of 2,870, the overall coefficient alpha was .91 and the overall test–restest reliability was .71. Table 4 indicates each of the JSS subscales and their corresponding reliability.

Table 4

Subscales, Alpha, and Reliability Indicators from the Job Satisfaction Survey

Scale	Items	Coefficient alpha	Test-retest reliability
Pay	1, 10, 19, 28	.75	.45
Promotion	2, 11, 20, 33	.73	.62
Supervision	3, 12, 21, 30	.82	.55
Fringe benefits	4, 13, 22, 29	.73	.37
Contingent rewards	5, 14, 23, 32	.76	.59
Operating procedures	6, 15, 24, 31	.62	.74
Coworkers	7, 16, 25, 34	.60	.64
Nature of work	8, 17, 27, 35	.78	.54
Communication	9, 18, 26, 36	.71	.65
Total		.91	.71

Note. From Spector's job satisfaction website. Copyright 1994 by Paul E. Spector, all rights reserved. Reprinted with permission.

Sample JSS questions. Participants were asked to rate 36 items based on a six-factor Likert-type scale where 1 indicated *disagree very much* and 6 indicated *agree very much*. The following five questions are samples of items from the JSS.

1. I do not feel that the work I do is appreciated.
2. I like doing the things I do at work.
3. I feel a sense of pride in doing my job.
4. I don't feel my efforts are rewarded the way they should be.
5. When I do a good job, I receive the recognition for it that I should receive.

Data Collection

A self-administered online survey was used as the method to collect data for the quantitative correlational study. According to Singleton and Straits (2010), surveys are widely accepted as an approach to social research, offer an effective means of social description, and have the potential to provide generalizing information about the larger population. In addition, online surveys provide a cost-effective means of reaching participants over a geographically dispersed area (Singleton & Straits, 2010). The survey included 36 job satisfaction items from the JSS, 36 items from the MLQ 5X for leadership style, personal demographic factors, and team-based demographic factors.

Potential participants received an e-mail inviting them to participate in the study. The e-mail explained the purpose of the study, the criteria for participation, the researcher's responsibilities regarding handling of data and maintaining the participants' anonymity, and a hyperlink to the actual study. The e-mail also asked participants to pass the e-mail to any colleagues who meet the study criteria. The study was created and housed at http://surveymethods.com. The survey remained open 3 weeks until the minimum sample size was achieved. After 1 week, a reminder e-mail was sent to potential participants.

Data Analysis

Data collected from the quantitative, correlational online survey was first checked for completeness. Surveys that were not complete were discarded. The data were then imported into SPSS 19.0 to determine if correlational relationships exist between SDM use, leadership style, and job satisfaction. According to Aczel and Sounderpandian (2009), researchers must be able to analyze the data statistically to make meaning from them and attempt to generalize rather than merely collect numerical data.

The strategy for analysis in the study was first to provide descriptive statistics by computing the mean, mode, median, and standard deviation of the demographic items. Then, a Pearson product–moment correlation test was performed to determine whether a relationship exists between SDM use, leadership style, and job satisfaction. The technique was referred to as product–moment because it uses standard deviation in its calculations. According to Balsley (1992), the advantage to using the Pearson product–moment is the use of standard deviation for both variables. The standard deviations were also used in calculating regression coefficients. A multiple regression analysis was performed to examine whether SDM use or leadership style can predict job satisfaction.

The measure of the linear relationship between two variables is the correlation between them (Aczel & Sounderpandian, 2009). The correlation between two variables is an indication of how well they move together in a straight line (Balsley, 1992; Miles & Shevlin, 2001). The indicator for how well two variables in a sample move together is called the correlation coefficient (r). The values for the correlation coefficient can range from -1 to +1, including 0 (Balsley, 1992; Miles & Shevlin, 2001). Aczel and Sounderpandian (2009) listed the value possibilities as follows:

1. If $r = 0$, then this indicates no correlation, or linear relationship, at all.

2. If $r = 1$, then there is a perfect, positive relationship or correlation between two variables. When one variable increases or decreases, the other variable does the same.

3. If $r = -1$, then there is a perfect, negative relationship. When one variable increases or decreases, the other variable does the opposite.

4. When r is between 0 and 1 or 0 and -1, then that number indicates the strength of the relationship between the two variables. A coefficient of .9 is considered positive and stronger than a .3.

In addition, the potential for Type I and II errors was addressed, so a p value was calculated and used in hypotheses testing to include a confidence level of .95.

Usefulness to the Field

The findings from the study provide valuable knowledge that may help IT project leaders to manage their software development projects more effectively. In addition, the study included relevant information regarding the potential effect of SDM use on IT personnel's job satisfaction. The literature review from chapter 2 provided insight into the types of research conducted in the area of SDMs. Much of the research for SDM use includes their importance in software development, the factors of method adoption, or which method is more effective. These factors are all based on an underlying assumption that the value of SDM use is in its link to project success and user satisfaction. The study of job satisfaction and voluntary turnover indicates there are important and somewhat unique factors to consider for IT personnel; however, researchers have not provided much linkage to IT personnel in IT project teams, specifically to those who use SDMs compared to those who do not. Thus, examining the correlation between SDM use, leadership style, and job satisfaction provided information useful to IT project leaders, organizations, and IT personnel.

Summary

Chapter 3 included a justification for utilizing a correlational design to examine the relationships between SDM use, leadership style, and job satisfaction. The data collection techniques and data analysis methods were outlined and justified as appropriate to answer the research questions. The instrument, an online survey, was also outlined to show that the appropriate strategy was utilized to obtain the information needed. Specifically, the survey gathered personal and team-based demographic information, utilized items from the MLQ 5X for leadership style information, and included items from the JSS for job satisfaction information. Data were analyzed using SPSS 19.0 software package. Data statistical methods included descriptive data such as mean, mode, median, and standard deviation as well as the Pearson product–moment correlation and regression analyses. In addition, the methods taken to ensure the ethical protection of participants were outlined to ensure adherence to the requirements set forth by the Walden University IRB.

Chapter 4 includes an explanation of the data analysis techniques used and contains the findings of the study, including the results of the hypotheses tests and a description of how the research questions were answered. Chapter 5 contains a discussion on the implications of the findings, the limitations of the study, recommendations for action, and recommendations for future research. Chapter 5 also includes an implication for social change.

Chapter 4: Data Analysis

The purpose of the quantitative study was to determine whether the use of SDMs was associated with IT employees having higher job satisfaction. A secondary purpose was to examine the relationship of leadership style between IT managers who use SDMs in IT projects and those who do not. The problem addressed in the study was whether the use of SDMs in IT projects influenced job satisfaction. Chapter 4 includes a detailed report of how the study was conducted, the data collection measures utilized, and how the data analysis was performed. Chapter 4 also includes an explanation of the results of the data analysis, including how the findings were used to test the hypotheses and to answer the research questions.

Data Collection Process

The sampling techniques for the study were a purposive sampling technique as well as snowball sampling. An introductory post was created that detailed pertinent information regarding the purpose of the study, inclusion criteria, a request for participants, and a hyperlink to access the anonymous Internet-based survey. The post was distributed to at least 50 IT-related groups from LinkedIn, a professional online networking website. In addition, at least 10 online IT forums were also utilized as a venue to distribute the introductory post. All participants were encouraged to forward the information to colleagues who met the criteria for participation.

The Internet-based survey included 84 items and 12 demographic questions. Thirty-six items were utilized to report respondents' attitudes on nine dimensions of job satisfaction. Thirty-six items were utilized to report respondents' perceptions on three leadership styles for their IT project leader. The survey remained open for 3 weeks and 287 respondents participated. A total of 192 participants did not finish the survey or did not meet the required criteria to continue and complete the survey. The resulting usable sample size was 95 participants, which was sufficient to meet the minimum sample size of 89 participants. A response rate could not be determined due to the anonymous nature of the survey and because the participants included IT persons from multiple organizations.

Analysis of Data

The questionnaire data were converted into an Excel spreadsheet format from http://SurveyMethods.com. The spreadsheet was then exported into SPSS 19.0 for analysis. Respondents' perceptions of leadership style for their IT project leader was measured using a validated and reliable 5-point Likert-type scale (1 = *not at all* to 5 = *frequently, if not always*) instrument. There were three leadership styles, transformational, transactional, and passive-avoidant, with each question assigned to a specific style. Transformational leadership style included 20 of the 36 total items (2, 6, 8, 9, 10, 13, 14, 15, 18, 19, 21, 23, 25, 26, 29, 30, 31, 32, 34, 36). Transactional leadership style included eight of the 36 total items (1, 4, 11, 16, 22, 24, 27, 35). Passive-avoidant leadership style also included eight of the 36 items (3, 5, 7, 12, 17, 20, 28, 33).

Respondents' job satisfaction was measured using a validated and reliable 6-point Likert-type scale (1 = *disagree very much* to 6 = *agree very much*) instrument. Nineteen of the 36 JSS items were negatively worded (2, 4, 6, 8, 10, 12, 14, 16, 18, 19, 21, 23, 24, 26, 29, 31, 32, 34, 36) and were reverse scored prior to analysis. Total job satisfaction consisted of nine subscales: pay, promotion, supervision, benefits, contingent rewards, operating conditions, coworkers, nature of work, and communication. Each of the subscales was addressed by four of the 36 JSS items.

Frequency distributions and descriptive statistics were performed to describe, organize, summarize, and present the raw data so that a profile of the study population could be established. Mean scores and standard deviations were calculated for transformational, transactional, and passive-avoidant leadership style scores as well as total job satisfaction and each of the JSS subscales. Correlation analyses were utilized to test the hypotheses. A *p* value of less than .05 was utilized to support the rejection of null hypotheses with a 95% confidence level. Backward elimination regression analyses were performed on all demographic items and variables to determine which items comprised the best models for potential predictability. The analysis results were reported in the following order:

1. Frequencies and percentages for demographic variables.
2. Means, standard deviations, and minimum and maximum values for demographic variables.
3. Psychometric characteristics of leadership style and job satisfaction results.
4. Hypothesis testing using Pearson product–moment correlations to determine the relationship between the variables.
5. Regression analyses.

Demographic Frequency and Percentage Results

The study survey included 12 major demographic items used to describe the characteristics of the respondents. Table 5 displays the overall frequency counts and percentages for the demographic items as well as the frequencies and percentages specific to both non-SDM users and SDM users. Overall, 56 of the respondents (58.9%) were SDM-users and 39 were non-SDM users (41.1%). About two thirds (68.4%) of the respondents were male and 31.6% were female. The median age range was 36-45 with five respondents in the age range of 18-25 (5.3%), 20 in the 26-35 range (21.1%), 27 in the 36-45 range (28.4%), 27 in the 46-55 range (28.4), and 16 in the 56 and older range (16.8%). Regarding the number of years at their organization, the median was 1- to 5- years. Nine respondents indicated less than 1 year (9.5%), 45 were in the 1- to 5-year range (47.4%), 14 were in the 6- to 10-year range (14.7%), and 27 were in the over 10-year range (28.4%). When asked to indicate the number of years in their current position, the median was over 10-years. Four respondents had less than 1 year (4.2%), 22 were in the 1- to 5-year range (23.2%), 18 were in the 6- to 10-year range (18.9%), and 51 were in the over 10-year range (53.7%).

The positions held by the respondents varied, but the majority self-identified as software developers or software testers. There were 27 software developers (28.4%), 20 quality assurance/testers (21.1%), seven database administrators (7.4%), six software analysts (6.3%), three software designers (3.2%), 14 software engineers (14.7%), five systems administrators (5.3%), and 13 in other positions (13.7%). Fifty-six (58.9%) of the projects were still ongoing, and 39 (41.1%) were considered finished. The majority of the projects (34.7%) were short having lasted 2-6 months. Of the remaining projects, 17.9% lasted 6-9 months, 13.7% lasted 9.-12 months, 18.9% lasted more than 12 months, and 14.7% lasted more than 24 months.

Table 5

Frequency Counts and Percentages for Demographic Variables (N = 95)

Variable and category	Non-SDM users		SDM users		Overall	
	n	%	*n*	%	*n*	%
Total participants	39	41.1	56	58.9	95	100.0
Gender						
Female	12	30.8	18	32.1	30	31.6
Male	27	69.2	38	67.9	65	68.4
Age range (years)						
18-25	0	0.0	5	8.9	5	5.3
26-35	12	30.8	8	14.3	20	21.1
36-45	9	23.1	18	32.1	27	28.4
46-55	10	25.6	17	30.4	27	28.4
56 and older	8	20.5	8	14.3	16	16.8
Years at organization						
< 1	2	5.1	7	12.5	9	9.5
1-5	23	59.0	22	39.3	45	47.4
6-10	1	2.6	13	23.2	14	14.7
> 10	13	33.3	14	25.0	27	28.4
Years in position						
< 1	0	0.0	4	7.1	4	4.2
1-5	13	33.3	9	16.1	22	23.2
6-10	5	12.8	13	23.2	18	18.9
> 10	21	53.8	30	53.6	51	53.7
Position						
Database administrator	3	7.7	4	7.1	7	7.4
Quality assurance/tester	4	10.3	16	28.6	20	21.1
Software analyst	2	5.1	4	7.1	6	6.3
Software designer	1	2.6	2	3.6	3	3.2
Software developer	13	33.3	14	25.0	27	28.4
Software engineer	7	17.9	7	12.5	14	14.7
Systems administrator	3	7.7	2	3.6	5	5.3
Other	6	15.4	7	12.5	13	13.7
Project status						
Finished	16	41.0	23	41.1	39	41.1
Ongoing	23	59.0	33	58.9	56	58.9
Project length						
2-6 months	16	41.0	17	30.4	33	34.7
6-9 months	7	17.9	10	17.9	17	17.9
9-12 months	3	7.7	10	17.9	13	13.7
>12 months	8	20.5	10	17.9	18	18.9
>24 months	5	12.8	9	16.1	14	14.7

Table 6 indicated that 41.1% of participants reported their IT software development team used no methodology. The remaining 58.9% of participants used a formal SDM with 27.4% using agile methods, 8.4% using rapid application development, 6.3% using waterfall, and 16.8% using other various methods.

Table 6

Frequency Counts and Percentages for Methodologies (N = 95)

Methodology	n	%
None	39	41.1
Agile methods	26	27.4
Rapid application development	8	8.4
Waterfall	6	6.3
Other	16	16.8

Descriptive Statistics

Table 7 shows the mean, standard deviation, low value, and high value for the number of team members. The lowest number of team members for both non-SDM users and SDM users was four members. The highest number of team members for non-SDM users was 25 persons, whereas the highest number of team members for SDM users was 60. The average number of team members for all participants was 10 ($M = 10.47$, $SD = 8.62$). The average number of team members for non-SDM users was eight ($M = 8.18$, $SD = 5.07$) and the average for SDM users was 12 ($M = 12.07$, $SD = 10.142$). These numbers indicate that software development teams generally tend to be smaller in IT shops that do not use a formal SDM.

Table 7

Descriptive Statistics for Number of Team Members (N = 95)

Variable and category	M	SD	Low	High
Non-SDM users	8.18	5.07	4	25
SDM users	12.07	10.14	4	60
All users	10.47	8.62	4	60

Participants' Job Satisfaction

Respondents' job satisfaction was measured using a validated and reliable 6-point Likert-type scale (1 = *disagree very much* to 6 = *agree very much*) instrument. The JSS includes 36 items separated into nine subscales.

According to Spector (1985), average scores of 4.00 and above represent satisfaction, average scores between 3.00 and 4.00 represent ambivalence, and scores below 3.00 represent dissatisfaction. Table 8 displays the psychometric characteristics for overall job satisfaction and the nine subscales. Total overall job satisfaction has a mean score of 3.90 ($SD = .87$). The subscales that had the highest means were supervision ($M = 4.54$, $SD = 1.41$), nature of work ($M = 4.65$, $SD = 1.06$), and coworkers ($M = 4.66$, $SD = .96$). The subscales that had the lowest means were promotion ($M = 3.17$, $SD = 1.13$), pay ($M = 3.38$, $SD = 1.23$), and operating conditions ($M = 3.62$, $SD = 1.13$). A Cronbach's alpha statistical test was used to test the internal reliability for all the responses. A Cronbach's alpha (α) score of greater than .70 indicates satisfactory reliability (Nakata & Zhu, 2007). The range for Cronbach's alpha was from $\alpha = .68$ to $\alpha = .91$ with a median $\alpha = .80$. The alpha coefficient for overall job satisfaction was $\alpha = .94$, which is higher than the reliability coefficient ($\alpha = .91$) reported by Spector (1985).

Table 8

Psychometric Characteristics for All Job Satisfaction Scores (N = 95)

Subscale	M	SD	Low	High	Alpha
Pay	3.38	1.23	1.00	6.00	.80
Promotion	3.17	1.13	1.00	6.00	.80
Supervision	4.54	1.41	1.00	6.00	.91
Benefits	3.68	1.19	1.00	6.00	.75
Contingent rewards	3.70	1.14	1.00	6.00	.73
Operating conditions	3.62	1.13	1.00	5.75	.68
Coworkers	4.66	0.96	2.00	6.00	.75
Nature of work	4.65	1.06	1.50	6.00	.84
Communication	3.69	1.26	1.00	6.00	.81
Total job satisfaction	3.90	0.87	1.00	5.56	.94

Tables 9 and 10 show the psychometric characteristics for job satisfaction for non-SDM users and SDM users separately. Table 9 indicates the mean for overall job satisfaction specific to non-SDM users was 3.70 (*SD* = .81). The subscales that had the highest means for non-SDM users were supervision (*M* = 4.51, *SD* = 1.30), nature of work (*M* = 4.47, *SD* = 1.05), and coworkers (*M* = 4.37, *SD* = 1.07). The subscales that had the lowest means were promotion (*M* = 2.78, *SD* = 1.01), pay (*M* = 3.22, *SD* = 1.22), and communication (*M* = 3.28, *SD* = 1.22).

Table 9

Psychometric Characteristics for Job Satisfaction Scores for Non-SDM Users (N = 39)

Subscale	M	SD	Low	High
Pay	3.22	1.22	1.00	5.50
Promotion	2.78	1.01	1.00	5.25
Supervision	4.51	1.30	1.25	6.00
Benefits	3.62	1.02	1.00	6.00
Contingent rewards	3.49	0.99	1.00	5.50
Operating conditions	3.55	1.23	1.00	5.25
Coworkers	4.37	1.07	2.00	6.00
Nature of work	4.47	1.05	1.50	6.00
Communication	3.28	1.22	1.00	5.75
Total job satisfaction	3.70	0.81	1.00	6.00

Table 10 indicates the mean for overall job satisfaction specific to SDM users was 4.04 (*SD* = .89). The subscales that had the highest means for SDM users were supervision (*M* = 4.57, *SD* = 1.50), nature of work (*M* = 4.78, *SD* = 1.06), and coworkers (*M* = 4.86, *SD* = .83). The subscales that had the lowest means were promotion (*M* = 3.44, *SD* = 1.14), pay (*M* = 3.50, *SD* = 1.24), and operating conditions (*M* = 3.68, *SD* = 1.07).

Table 10

Psychometric Characteristics for Job Satisfaction Scores for SDM Users (N = 56)

Subscale	*M*	*SD*	Low	High
Pay	3.50	1.24	1.00	6.00
Promotion	3.44	1.14	1.00	6.00
Supervision	4.57	1.50	1.00	6.00
Benefits	3.73	1.31	1.00	6.00
Contingent rewards	3.85	1.21	1.00	6.00
Operating conditions	3.68	1.07	1.00	5.75
Coworkers	4.86	0.83	2.00	6.00
Nature of work	4.78	1.06	2.00	6.00
Communication	3.98	1.22	1.00	6.00
Total job satisfaction	4.04	0.89	1.00	6.00

A comparison of psychometric characteristics for overall job satisfaction for non-SDM users and SDM users indicated one major difference. The mean score for overall job satisfaction for the SDM-user subsample was 4.04, which according to Spector (1985) is in the satisfaction range. The mean overall job satisfaction score for the non-SDM user subsample was 3.70, which is in the ambivalent range. The only mean score that fell into the dissatisfaction range was for the subscale promotion (*M* = 2.78) for non-SDM users.

Participants' Perceptions of Leadership Style

Respondents' perceptions of leadership style for their IT project leader was measured using a validated and reliable 5-point Likert-type scale (0 = *not at all* to 4 = *frequently, if not always*) instrument. This study utilized Avolio and Bass's (2004) model three correlated factors (transformational vs. transactional vs. passive-avoidant leadership) to measure these three factors as leadership styles. Each of the three leadership style factors consisted of specific questions averaged for an overall score specific to that leadership style. Table 11 shows the mean score for transformational leadership style for all participants was 2.15 (*SD* =.86) with a Cronbach's alpha coefficient of α = .95. Transactional leadership style had a mean score of 1.92 (*SD* = .68) with an alpha of α = .71. Passive-avoidant leadership style had a mean score of 1.23 (*SD* = .93) and an alpha of α = .90.

Table 11

Psychometric Characteristics for Leadership Styles for All (N = 95)

Leadership style	*M*	*SD*	Low	High	Alpha
Transformational	2.15	0.86	.30	3.65	.95
Transactional	1.92	0.68	.25	3.63	.71
Passive-avoidant	1.23	0.93	.00	3.63	.90

Tables 12 and 13 detail the psychometric characteristics for leadership style for non-SDM users and SDM users separately. For non-SDM users specifically, Table 12 shows the mean score for transformational leadership style for all participants was 1.91 (*SD* =.79). Transactional leadership style had a mean score of 1.75 (*SD* = .71). Passive-avoidant leadership style had a mean score of 1.38 (*SD* = .87).

Table 12

Psychometric Characteristics for Leadership Styles for Non-SDM Users (N = 39)

Leadership style	*M*	*SD*	Low	High
Transformational	1.91	0.79	.30	3.45
Transactional	1.75	0.71	.25	3.63

Passive-avoidant	1.38	0.87	.13	3.25

Table 13 indicated that specific to SDM users, the mean score for transformational leadership style for all participants was 2.32 (*SD* =.88). Transactional leadership style had a mean score of 2.05 (*SD* = .50). Passive-avoidant leadership style had a mean score of 1.13 (*SD* = .96).

Table 13

Psychometric Characteristics for Leadership Styles for SDM Users (N = 56)

Leadership style	*M*	*SD*	Low	High
Transformational	2.32	0.88	.35	3.65
Transactional	2.05	0.50	.50	3.25
Passive-avoidant	1.13	0.96	.00	3.63

A comparison of psychometric characteristics for leadership styles for non-SDM users versus SDM users indicated some difference. The mean scores for transformational and transactional leadership styles for SDM users (*M* = 2.32 and *M* = 2.05, respectively) are higher than the scores for non-SDM users (*M* = 1.91 and *M* = 1.75, respectively). However, the mean score for passive-avoidant leadership style was higher for non-SDM users (*M* = 1.38) than the mean score for SDM users (*M* = 1.13).

Data Analysis and Results

Research Question 1

The first research question was as follows: What is the relationship, if any, between formal SDM use and overall job satisfaction? To address this question, a null hypothesis (There is no relationship between formal SDM use and overall job satisfaction for IT software development team members) was created. A Pearson product–moment correlation was performed on overall SDM use and overall job satisfaction to determine whether a statistically significant relationship exists between the two variables. Table

14 indicates that the correlation coefficient was $r = .20$ ($p = .06$), which suggests a weak positive relationship between overall SDM use and overall job satisfaction. The p value of .06 is not lower than the 5% level of significance, indicating that no significant correlation was sufficient to reject the null hypothesis. Thus, no statistically significant relationship exists between SDM use and overall job satisfaction.

Table 14 also displays the correlation coefficients between the job satisfaction subscales and overall SDM use. Three of nine job satisfaction subscales had positive, statistically significant correlations with overall SDM use: (a) promotion ($r = .29$, $p = .004$), (b) coworkers ($r = .25$, $p = .01$), and (c) communication ($r = .28$, $p = .007$). These coefficients indicate that SDM use tends to be associated with higher satisfaction with opportunities for promotion, good relationships with coworkers, and good team communication. Table 14 indicates that the other six job satisfaction subscales had weak positive correlations with SDM use, but those correlations were not considered statistically significant.

Research Question 2

The second research question was as follows: What is the relationship, if any, between leadership style of leaders who are SDM users versus leaders who are non-SDM users and overall job satisfaction? To address this question, a null hypothesis (There is no difference in the relationship between leadership style of leaders who use SDM versus leaders who do not use SDM and overall job satisfaction for IT software development team members) was created. A Pearson product–moment correlation analysis was performed on overall SDM use, the three leadership styles, and overall job satisfaction to determine if a statistically significant relationship existed between the variables.

Table 14

Pearson Product-Moment Correlation Between SDM Use and Job Satisfaction Subscales

(N = 95)

Scale	Overall SDM-use[a]
Total job satisfaction	.20
Pay	.11
Promotion	.29***
Supervision	.02
Benefits	.04
Contingent rewards	.15
Operating conditions	.06
Coworkers	.25*
Nature of work	.15
Communication	.28**

[a] SDM coding: 0 = no, 1 = yes.
* $p < .05$. ** $p < .01$. *** $p < .01$.

Table 15 indicates that the correlation coefficient for overall SDM use was $r = .20$ ($p = .06$), which indicates a weak positive relationship between SDM use and overall job satisfaction. For transformational leadership style, the correlation coefficient was $r = .72$ ($p = .001$). For transactional leadership style, the correlation coefficient was $r = .50$ ($p = .001$). These correlation coefficients indicated a strong positive relationship for all participants for both transformational and transactional leadership styles and overall job satisfaction. For passive-avoidant leadership style, the correlation coefficient was $r = -.67$ ($p = .001$). This correlation coefficient indicates a strong negative relationship for all participants between passive-avoidant leadership style and overall job satisfaction. For all three leadership styles $p = .001$, which means the relationships were also statistically significant.

Table 15

Correlation Between SDM Use, Leadership Styles, and Job Satisfaction (N = 95)

Scale	*1*	*2*	*3*	*4*	*5*
1. Job satisfaction	1.00				
2. Overall SDM use	.20	1.00			
3. Transformational	.72**	.23*	1.00		

4. Transactional	.50**	.24*	.69**	1.00
5. Passive-avoidant	-.67**	-.13	-.63**	-.44**	1.00

*p < .05 **p < .01*

In addition, Table 15 indicated that overall SDM use is positively, significantly related to transformational leadership style ($r = .23, p = .02$) and transactional leadership style ($r = .24, p = .03$). However, overall SDM use was weakly and negatively, but not significantly, related to passive-avoidant leadership style ($r = -.13, p = .21$). These coefficients indicated that SDM use tends to be related to both the transformational and transactional leadership styles, but passive-avoidant leadership is not necessarily related to non-SDM use.

Tables 16 and 17 show the correlations for the three leadership styles and overall job satisfaction separated by non-SDM user and SDM user. For the non-SDM user subsample, Table 16 indicates that transformational leadership style ($r = .62, p = .001$) and transactional leadership style ($r = .51, p = .001$) have strong positive relationships with overall job satisfaction. Passive-avoidant leadership style ($r = -.72. p = .001$) has a strong, reverse correlation with overall job satisfaction. Additionally, all three leadership styles have statistically significant relationships with overall job satisfaction for non-SDM users.

Table 16
Correlation Between Leadership Styles and Job Satisfaction for Non-SDM Users (N = 39)

Scale	Overall job satisfaction*
Transformational	.62
Transactional	.51
Passive-avoidant	-.72

* *p < .01*

Specific to the SDM user subsample, Table 17 indicates that both transformational leadership style ($r = .75, p = .001$) and transactional leadership style ($r = .47, p = .001$) have strong positive relationships with overall job satisfaction. Passive-avoidant leadership style ($r = -.63. p = .001$) has a strong, negative correlation with overall job satisfaction. Additionally, all three leadership styles have statistically significant relationships with overall job satisfaction for SDM users.

Table 17
Correlation Between Leadership Styles and Job Satisfaction for SDM Users (N = 56)

Scale	Overall job satisfaction
Transformational	.75**
Transactional	.47**
Passive-Avoidant	-.63**

** p < .01

A comparison between the correlations for the three leadership styles and overall job satisfaction for non-SDM users versus SDM users indicated some differences. Even though both groups have strong positive correlations considered to be statistically significant, the correlation coefficient for transformational leadership style is higher for SDM users ($r = .75$) than for non-SDM users ($r = .62$). These coefficients indicated that a stronger relationship exists between job satisfaction and perceptions of transformational leadership style for IT leaders when a formal SDM is used. When a formal SDM is used and the leader is perceived as having a transformational leadership style, job satisfaction is likely to be higher than when a formal SDM is not used.

Additionally, even though both groups have strong negative correlations that are considered statistically significant, the correlation coefficient for passive-avoidant leadership style is higher for non-SDM users ($r = -.72$) than for SDM users ($r = -.63$). These coefficients indicated a stronger relationship exists between job satisfaction and perceptions of passive-avoidant leadership for IT leaders when a formal SDM is not used. When a formal SDM is not used and the leader is perceived as having a passive-avoidant leadership style, job satisfaction is likely to be lower than when a formal SDM is used. Because of these differences in the correlation coefficients between SDM users and non-SDM users and because the *p* values of .001 were lower than the 5% level of significance in all cases, these factors indicated sufficient reason to reject the null hypothesis.

Other Findings

To determine if any predictability potential existed for the dependent variable overall job satisfaction based on overall SDM use, leadership style, and any demographic items, backward elimination regressions were performed. According to Aczel and Sounderpandian (2009), during a backward elimination regression, all the variables are included in the first model. The variable with the least significance is removed and the regression is rerun. This procedure repeats until only variables with the most significance remain. The remaining variables make up a model that has the most power to explain the variances in the dependent variable.

Table 18 displays the results of a backward elimination regression model that predicted overall job satisfaction based on demographic items only. For all participants ($N = 95$), the final model was statistically significant ($p = .008$) and accounted for 9.9% of the variance in the dependent variable. Specifically, higher job satisfaction was negatively related to the number of team members ($\beta = -.25, p = .02$) and positively related to overall SDM use ($\beta = .25, p = .014$), which indicates job satisfaction is higher when a formal SDM is used along with smaller teams. For the SDM user subsample ($n = 56$), the final model was statistically significant ($p = .044$) and accounted for 7.3% of the variance in the dependent variable. Specifically, job satisfaction was negatively related to the number of team members ($\beta = -0.27, p = .044$), which also supported the previously discussed model indicating that under conditions of SDM use, smaller teams tend to be related to higher job satisfaction. For the non-SDM user subsample ($n = 39$), the final model was statistically significant ($p = .100$) and accounted for 7.2% of the variance in the dependent variable. Specifically, job satisfaction was positively related to the number of years in position ($\beta = 0.27, p = .100$), which means for non-SDM users, job satisfaction tended to be higher for those who had been in their position longer.

Table 19 shows the results for backward elimination regression models that predicted overall job satisfaction based on demographic items and leadership style. For all participants ($N = 95$), the final model was statistically significant ($p = .001$) and accounted for 60.8% of the variance in the dependent variable. Specifically, job satisfaction was positively related to gender ($\beta = -.11$, $p = .09$), positively related to the transformational leadership score ($\beta = .49$, $p = .001$), and negatively related to the passive-avoidant leadership score ($\beta = -.36$, $p = .001$). These findings indicated that job satisfaction tends to be higher when the IT worker is a woman whose perceptions of transformational leadership is higher and whose passive-avoidant leadership is lower.

Table 18

Prediction of Job Satisfaction Based on Demographic Items

Variable	B	SE	β	p
Overall SDM sample ($N = 95$) [a]				
Intercept	3.90	0.16		.001
Team members	-0.03	0.01	-0.25	.015
SDM use	0.44	0.18	0.25	.014
SDM use ($n = 56$) [b]				
Intercept	4.33	0.18		.001
Team members	-0.02	0.01	-0.27	.044
Non-SDM users ($n = 39$) [c]				
Intercept	2.95	0.46		.001
Years in position	0.23	0.14	0.27	.100

[a] Final model: $F(2,92) = 5.04$, $p = .008$. $R^2 = .099$. Candidate variables = 8.
[b] Final model: $F(1,54) = 4.27$, $p = .044$. $R^2 = .073$. Candidate variables = 7.
[c] Final model: $F(1,37) = 2.85$, $p = .100$. $R^2 = .072$. Candidate variables = 7.

Table 19

Prediction of Job Satisfaction Based on Demographic Items and Leadership Style

Variable	B	SE	β	p
Overall sample ($N = 95$) [a]				
Intercept	3.40	0.28		.001
Gender [b]	-0.21	0.12	-0.11	.09
Transformational	0.49	0.09	0.49	.001
Passive-avoidant	-0.33	0.08-0.36		.001
SDM use ($n = 56$) [c]				
Intercept	2.93	0.35		.001
Transformational	0.60	0.11	0.59	.001
Passive-avoidant	-0.24	0.10	-0.26	.02
Non-SDM users ($n = 39$) [d]				
Intercept	3.84	0.42		.001
Transformational	0.29	0.14	0.28	.05
Passive-avoidant	-0.51	0.13	-0.55	.001

[a] Final model: $F(3,91) = 47.05$, $p = .001$. $R^2 = .608$. Candidate variables = 11.
[b] Gender: 0 = *female*, 1 = *male*.
[c] Final model: $F(2,53) = 41.21$, $p = .001$. $R^2 = .609$. Candidate variables = 10.
[d] Final model: $F(2,36) = 24.13$, $p = .001$. $R^2 = .573$. Candidate variables = 10.

For the SDM users subsample ($n = 56$), the final model was statistically significant ($p = .001$) and accounted for 60.9% of the variance in the dependent variable. Specifically, job satisfaction was positively related to the transformational leadership score ($\beta = .59$, $p = .001$) and negatively related to the passive-avoidant leadership score ($\beta = -.26$, $p = .022$). For the non-SDM users subsample ($n = 39$), the final model was statistically significant ($p = .001$) and accounted for 57.3% of the variance in the dependent variable. Specifically, job satisfaction was positively related to the transformational leadership score ($\beta = 0.28$, $p = .050$) and negatively related to the passive-avoidant leadership score ($\beta = -.55$, $p = .001$). Scores for both models indicated that regardless of whether there is a formal SDM used, job satisfaction is higher when perceptions of transformational leadership is higher and passive-avoidant leadership is lower.

Summary

The problem addressed in the study was whether job satisfaction was influenced by the use of formal SDMs in IT projects. Participants included IT personnel involved in software development teams of at least four members having worked on IT projects lasting at least 2 months. IT project leaders were not included in the study. The data were imported from http://SurveyMethods.com into an Excel spreadsheet and then into SPSS 19.0 for analysis. Frequency distributions and descriptive statistics were performed to determine the demographic characteristics of the sample. Of the 95 total respondents, 56 (58.9%) used a formal SDM and 39 (41.1%) did not use an SDM at all. The average team size for SDM users was 12 ($M =$ 12.07, $SD = 10.14$), and for non-SDM users, the average team size was eight ($M = 8.18$, $SD = 5.07$). A Pearson product–moment analysis was performed to examine the relationship between SDM use and overall job satisfaction. The correlation coefficient was $r = .20$ ($p = .06$), which failed to reject the null hypothesis. The average job satisfaction score for SDM users was 4.04 and for non-SDM users was 3.70, which indicates some difference between the two groups; however, the findings from the correlation analysis supported that no statistically significant relationship exists between SDM use and overall job satisfaction.

A Pearson product–moment analysis was performed to examine whether a relationship exists between leadership style and overall job satisfaction for SDM users versus non-SDM users. The correlation coefficient for SDM users for transformational leadership style was $r = .75$ ($p = .001$), transactional leadership style was $r = .47$ ($p = .001$), and passive-avoidant leadership style was $r = -.63$ ($p = .001$). The correlation coefficient for non-SDM users for transformational leadership style was $r = .62$ ($p = .001$), transactional leadership style was $r = .51$ ($p = .001$), and passive-avoidant leadership style was $r = -.72$ ($p = .001$). Because correlations for all leadership styles were significant and because there were differences between SDM users and non-SDM users, Null Hypothesis 2 was rejected.

Chapter 5 contains an interpretation of the research findings. Additionally, the chapter includes an explanation of the limitations of the study, recommendations for practitioners, and suggestions for future research. The chapter concludes with a discussion of implications for social change.

Chapter 5: Summary, Conclusion, and Recommendations

Overview

The purpose of the quantitative study was to determine whether the use of SDMs is associated with IT employees having higher job satisfaction. A secondary purpose was to examine the relationship of job satisfaction and the leadership style of IT managers who use SDMs in IT projects versus those who do not. Current research indicated that theorists have approached SDM use from many different perspectives with the underlying assumption that the value of SDM use is in project success and user satisfaction. In support of the sociotechnical theoretical framework, the study involved examining SDM use from the perspective of social or human aspects. Specifically, SDM use, perceptions of project leaders' leadership style, and their relationship to IT personnel's job satisfaction were examined.

Chapter 4 included a report of how the data analysis was performed as well as the findings from the study. Chapter 5 includes a summary and interpretation of the findings including limitations, implications, and recommendations for future research. Specifically, chapter 5 will include the following: summary and interpretation of findings, limitations of current study, recommendations for future research, recommendations for action, implications for social change, and conclusion.

Summary and Interpretation of Findings

The sample size for the study was 95 participants who self-identified as being part of an IT software development team having at least four members and working on an IT project lasting at least 2 months. The average team size for SDM users was 12 members and for non-SDM users, the average team size was eight members, which may indicate that organizational leaders tend to use SDMs when IT projects call for larger teams. Fifty-nine percent of the participants indicated that they use a formal SDM. This finding is similar to the G. Fitzgerald et al. (1999) study that indicated only 57% of the IT systems development persons surveyed utilized a formal SDM. Regarding project length, 41% of the projects for non-SDM users lasted 2–6 months and 30 % of the projects for SDM users lasted 2–6 months. This finding indicates that organizations with longer and more complex IT projects tend to use SDMs. One third of the participants were female and two thirds were male. The collected data were analyzed to form a demographic profile of the respondents as well as to test the hypotheses and to answer the research questions. A p value of .05 was used to support rejecting the null hypothesis at a 95% confidence level. The rest of this section provides an interpretation of the data analysis findings from chapter 4.

Research Question 1

The first research question investigated the relationship between formal SDM use and overall job satisfaction. To address this question, Null Hypothesis 1 was created, which stated that no relationship exists between formal SDM use and overall job satisfaction for IT software development team members. This hypothesis was tested using a Pearson product–moment correlation analysis. The results ($r = .20$, $p = .06$) were not sufficient to support the existence of a relationship. The p value of .06 was greater than the .05 significance level, which indicated the results failed to reject the null hypothesis. Additionally, $R^2 = .038$, which indicated that only 3.8% of the variance of overall job satisfaction can be explained by overall SDM use.

In looking at the job satisfaction subscales, a significant relationship existed between SDM use and three of the nine JSS subscales. The subscales were promotion ($r = .29$, $p = .004$), (b) coworkers ($r = .25$, $p = .013$), and (c) communication ($r = .28$, $p = .007$). These findings indicated that for IT personnel, overall SDM use was associated with perceptions of promotion opportunities, coworkers' relationships within the software development team, and overall team communication. These findings were similar to a study by Pedrycz et al. (2010), indicating that factors such as communication and work environment all positively relate to job satisfaction under conditions of agile programming used as a formal SDM. Similarly, Sanchez (2010) found work environment had a strong relationship with job satisfaction for IT professional employees.

While the Pearson product–moment correlation analysis failed to support a significant relationship between SDM use and overall job satisfaction, a comparison of the average job satisfaction score for SDM users versus non-SDM users indicated there is some difference. The mean score for overall job satisfaction for SDM users was 4.04, which according to Spector (1985) is in the satisfaction range. The mean overall job satisfaction score for non-SDM users was 3.70, which is in the ambivalent range. One possible explanation is that although these differences indicate SDM users, in general, have a higher job satisfaction than non-SDM users, other factors may need to be considered to present a significant correlation.

A backward elimination regression was performed to determine if there was any explaining power for the dependent variable overall job satisfaction based on overall SDM use and demographic items. The results indicated that team size ($\beta = -.25$, $p = .015$) and being in an SDM environment ($\beta = .25$, $p = .014$) explained 9.9% of the variance in job satisfaction. In essence, job satisfaction will likely be higher when respondents are in smaller teams and work in an SDM environment. One possible explanation is that while SDM use alone is not significantly correlated to overall job satisfaction, adding other factors to the analysis may result in a significant correlation.

Research Question 2

The topic of the second research question was the relationship between leadership style of leaders who are SDM users versus leaders who are non-SDM users and overall job satisfaction. To address this question, Null Hypothesis 2 was created, which stated that no difference exists in the relationship between leadership style of leaders who use SDM versus leaders who do not use SDM and overall job satisfaction for IT software development team members. This hypothesis was first tested using a Pearson product–moment correlation analysis on overall SDM use, the three leadership styles, and overall job satisfaction. The results again indicated that the correlation for overall SDM use ($r = .20$, $p = .06$) was not sufficient to support the existence of a relationship. However, for transformational leadership style, the correlation coefficient was $r = .72$ ($p = .001$) and for passive-avoidant leadership style, the correlation coefficient was $r = -.67$ ($p = .001$). These coefficients and p values indicated sufficient evidence existed to support the existence of a relationship.

A Pearson product–moment correlation analysis was then performed separately for SDM and non-SDM user subsamples. The results indicated that for SDM users, transformational leadership style ($r = .75$, $p = .001$) had a positive significant correlation with job satisfaction and passive-avoidant leadership style ($r = -.63$. $p = .001$) had a strong, reverse correlation with job satisfaction. For non-SDM users, transformational leadership style ($r = .62$, $p = .001$) had a positive significant correlation with job satisfaction and passive-avoidant leadership style ($r = -.72$. $p = .001$) had a strong, reverse correlation with job satisfaction. A comparison of the coefficients indicated a stronger relationship existed between transformational leadership style and job satisfaction for SDM users over non-SDM users. The comparison also indicated a stronger negative relationship existed between passive-avoidant leadership style and job satisfaction for non-SDM users over SDM users. Because of these differences in the correlation coefficients between SDM users and non-SDM users and because the p values of .001 were lower than the 5% level of significance in all cases, these factors indicated sufficient reason to reject the null hypothesis.

The result of the study indicating that transformational, transactional, and passive-avoidant leadership styles are significantly related to job satisfaction is not surprising. For example, Bodla and Nawaz (2010) indicated that transformational leadership was related to job satisfaction. In a meta-analysis, Dum dum, Lowe, and Avolio (2002) found that transformational leadership was consistently associated with having a higher positive effect on job satisfaction over transactional leadership, which had a higher positive effect on job satisfaction over passive-avoidant leadership. Additionally, Watson (2009) indicated that passive-avoidant leadership is negatively related to job satisfaction.

Although the correlation analysis results failed to indicate a significant relationship between overall SDM use, leadership style, and job satisfaction, obvious differences exist in the data. Psychometric characteristics indicate that the mean score for transformational leadership style for non-SDM users ($M = 1.91$) is lower than the mean score for SDM users ($M = 2.32$). In addition, the mean score for passive-avoidant leadership style for non-SDM users ($M = 1.38$) is higher than SDM users ($M = 1.13$). One possible explanation is that respondents who use SDMs in general tend to perceive their IT leaders as possessing a more transformational leadership style, whereas non-SDM users tend to view their IT leaders as having a more passive-avoidant leadership style.

A backward elimination regression was performed to determine if any explaining power existed for the dependent variable overall job satisfaction based on overall SDM use, leadership style, and demographic items. The resulting model indicated that gender ($\beta = .11$, $p = .089$), transformational leadership style ($\beta = .049$, $p = .001$), and passive-avoidant leadership style ($\beta = -.036$, $p = .001$) explained 60.8% of the variance in job satisfaction. Overall job satisfaction tends to be higher when the respondent is female, perceptions of transformational leadership style are higher, and perceptions of passive-avoidant leadership style are lower.

Interestingly, the results for backward elimination regression for job satisfaction based on leadership style and demographic items, but separating SDM users and non-SDM users, produced two models that included both transformational and passive-avoidant leadership styles. The results for SDM users indicated that transformational leadership style (β = .59, p = .001) and passive-avoidant leadership style (β = -.26, p = .022) explained 60.9% of the variance in job satisfaction. For non-SDM users, the results indicated that transformational leadership style (β = .28, p = .050) and passive-avoidant leadership style (β = -.55, p = .001) explained 57.3% of the variance in job satisfaction.

A comparison of these two models indicated that transformational leadership style has a higher positive effect on job satisfaction for SDM users over non-SDM users. For non-SDM users, passive-avoidant leadership style has a higher negative effect on job satisfaction than SDM users. One possible explanation is that job satisfaction for respondents who use SDMs tends to be more reliant on their IT leader having a transformational leadership style. Transformational leadership style for non-SDM users has less of an effect on their job satisfaction level, which indicates SDM use has a small effect on job satisfaction. The same conclusion applies to passive-avoidant leadership style. Passive-avoidant leadership style has a higher negative effect on non-SDM users. For respondents who use SDMs, the effect of passive-avoidant leadership style is lower than non-SDM users, which indicates that SDM users may have higher job satisfaction even when their IT project leader is perceived as having a passive-avoidant leadership style.

Based on the results of the study, overall SDM use alone has a limited relationship with job satisfaction. A strong relationship exists between the three leadership styles and job satisfaction; however, SDM use adds little to explain overall job satisfaction. Some minor differences indicate overall job satisfaction in general may be higher for SDM users; however, because there is no statistical significance, other unidentified factors may need to be investigated. In addition, the regression models for SDM users versus non-SDM users both indicate transformational leadership style and passive-avoidant leadership style are predictors of job satisfaction with slight differences in levels of effect and significance.

Limitations of Current Study

As is true with any research project, the quantitative, correlational study had some important limitations that need to be discussed. The first limitation was due to the methodological approach to the study. According to Simon (2006), although correlation and regression may be used to examine relationships between variables, causation cannot be determined. Quantitative studies are used to gather numerical data that may be generalized back to a population; however, utilizing a qualitative design would have provided more context-rich information regarding the influence of SDM use on IT personnel's job satisfaction.

The second limitation involves the determination of the target participant pool. Purposive and snowball sampling techniques were used for the study to reach the desired participants. In addition, online professional venues were targeted to request participation. Other techniques, such as partnering with specific organizations based on organization size, industry, shop size, and so forth, may have produced different results. In addition, the survey contained no questions to identify the type of industry or whether the organization was in the private or public sector. This information would have been helpful for generalization purposes.

Recommendations for Future Research

As previously discussed, little research exists regarding the effect of SDM use specific to IT personnel. This study provided a starting point, but more work is needed in this area. The results of the study indicated that SDM use alone has little effect on overall job satisfaction; however, the introduction of other factors may provide more insight into the relationship between SDM use and job satisfaction. Future researchers may want to include a more stratified random sample to ensure specific demographics are obtained. For example, whether the respondents' organizations were private, public, or governmental was not known in the current study. Whether the respondents were evenly distributed across several industries was not known. The organization size was not known. Creating a study that ensures the inclusion of a wide range of organizations might produce different results that are better generalized to IT.

Although the survey in the study met the requirements for answering the research questions and testing the hypotheses, utilizing other data collection methods may have provided more contextual information. Open-ended questions could be utilized to obtain richer information about the organization's culture, the makeup of the software development teams, and the project dynamics. For some organizations, larger, more complex IT projects may be more common. For other organizations, larger, more complex projects may occur only once a year. Whether the projects are primarily for external or internal customers may also be a contributing factor. Even though the respondents indicated whether their IT project was finished or ongoing and the length of the project, the end date for finished projects was not requested. A project ending 11 months ago compared to one ending 1 month ago may elicit different responses regarding perceptions of leadership style and job satisfaction.

In the current study, respondents were asked whether their IT project leaders utilized formal SDMs. Future researchers may also elicit more information from those who do not use formal SDMs to determine if the IT project leader manages projects in a manner similar to using a formal SDM. The IT project leader may have developed an informal SDM based on personal experience and the needs of the organization. In this scenario, IT personnel reap the benefits of effective software development project management without knowledge of using a formal SDM. Additionally, other factors may need to be examined to determine the relationship between

SDM use and job satisfaction. For example, in addition to the factors already mentioned, the team member's individual personality type may play a role.

Even though the MLQ (5X) is a valid and reliable instrument to measure transformational, transactional, and passive-avoidant leadership, the premise of the study was that each of these three categories may be examined as a leadership style. However, leadership styles can be operationalized in many other ways. Future researchers might utilize other instruments that measure differing constructs of leadership style to determine their relationship, if any, with SDM use and job satisfaction.

Finally, as the researcher for the study did not control for factors such as organization size, industry, organization type, team size, and so forth, future researchers who wish to conduct a similar quantitative study may want to expand their sample size to ensure the ability to generalize to the broader IT software development population. Future researchers may also want to perform a case study to examine an organization's practices more in-depth as a formal SDM is adopted and implemented.

Recommendations for Action

As discussed previously, a high percentage of IT projects are categorized as being not successful, ranging from failed and abandoned to challenged (Frolick et al., 2007; Standish Group, 2010). The reasons for failed projects is varied, but the top factors that led to the success of IT projects included executive management support, project management expertise, the use of formalized methodologies, and the adoption of agile processes (Standish Group, 2010). Much of the empirical research to date indicates that the focus of researchers and practitioners has been on project success and user satisfaction. Very little research has addressed the effect of the adoption and use of SDMs on IT personnel and job satisfaction. The importance of IT software development projects should be viewed from multiple perspectives, not just traditional measurements of project success.

Thus, organizational leaders should take steps to consider all factors that may play a role in project success.

Other empirical research indicates that job dissatisfaction is an antecedent to voluntary turnover (Lambert et al., 2001). Voluntary turnover is an important concern in organizations, in terms of both the cost of hiring and training employees and the loss of knowledge (Kempaiah & Luftman, 2007). Knowledge attrition can be a crucial concern when employees work in technical fields. Thus, it is especially important for IT leaders to be cognizant of factors that can cause voluntary turnover in organizations that are heavily reliant on IT activities in their organizational change endeavors as well as the products and services offered to customers.

Empirical research has also indicated that within organizations, the decision to adopt an SDM involves different factors including the technical requirements and the needs of IT personnel (Hansen et al., 2004; Livermore, 2008). In many cases, organizational leaders are resistant to adopting SDMs for various reasons. Two specific aspects of resistance include the claim that SDMs are not tailored to meet specific project and organizational needs and that SDMs do not fit well with the social needs of a development team or the organization (Bajec & Vavpotic, 2009). While current research already highlighted a connection between SDM use and the development team, much more research is needed to understand this connection from other perspectives. This realization also supports the idea that when making a strategic decision regarding the adoption of a formal SDM, organizational leaders should look beyond their traditional view of IT projects based almost solely on project success factors or user satisfaction. In fact, organizations should adopt a broader view of success factors that recognizes all project stakeholders including IT personnel. Thus, project success should be measured in terms of stakeholder satisfaction, not just end-user satisfaction.

Even though the study indicated that SDM use has a limited relationship with job satisfaction, the results add to the existing body of knowledge that organizational and IT project leaders should consider when making the decision to adopt a formal SDM. For example, the results indicated that team size and the number of years in a position are also factors that should be considered. Therefore, from an organizational change perspective, in an effort to decide whether to adopt a formal SDM, as IT leaders evaluate the needs of the organization as well as the requirements for projects and the end users, attention should also be paid to factors, or a combination of factors, that may affect IT personnel, including their job satisfaction. The results of the current study may be useful for IT leaders and managers in developing strategies that will ultimately improve the process of software development as well as managing projects successfully.

Implications for Social Change

The results of the study may affect social change by providing IT project leaders and organizational leaders with the information needed to make better strategic decisions that could potentially affect job satisfaction and reduce turnover intention for IT personnel. As discussed in chapter 2, previous research involving SDMs in IT projects has provided support for their use, indicating that they provide consistency, quality-checked deliverables, and an engineering-like discipline to IT projects (Cray, 2009; Fields et al., 1998). However, in practical terms, some reluctance by IT leaders and software developers to use them still exists (Livermore, 2008).

The introduction of new avenues of research, especially those that investigate the relationship between SDM use and its effect on IT personnel specifically, have the potential to enhance the ability for leaders to make decisions strategic to the organization as a whole. These new avenues provide IT project leaders and organizational leaders with information that supports SDM use not only for traditional reasons, such as project success and user satisfaction, but also for alternative reasons based on the needs of those IT personnel involved in the IT projects. This perspective is in support of the sociotechnical theoretical framework utilized in the current study that not only called for providing a sufficient technical subsystem, but also for providing for a social subsystem that considers the social or human characteristics of a software development team.

Although more efficient and successfully managed IT projects may arguably lead to increased user satisfaction, which has historically been a primary consideration in organizations, other stakeholders have been largely ignored in the process. IT personnel are also project stakeholders in IT projects. Thus, the results of the current study, as well as the investigation into formal practices such as SDM use and their potential influence on job satisfaction, have the capacity to affect IT personnel by increasing stakeholder satisfaction, promoting healthier project environments, and improving overall working conditions. These factors may all play an important role in job satisfaction and ultimately decrease voluntary turnover for IT personnel.

In sum, the current research study not only provides information that adds to the overall body of knowledge, but also adds practical information that may help organizational leaders to make better strategic decisions for their IT departments and projects. In addition, this study provides an enhanced ability for IT project leaders to manage projects more effectively and efficiently, while still considering the needs of IT personnel who work in software development teams. The ability of organizational leaders to make better, more informed decisions based on the newest research may have an industry-wide effect resulting in a shift in best practices for organizations, especially those in technology-based industries.

Conclusion

For many organizations, the successful completion of IT projects is crucial to their ability to function, to meet the needs of both internal and external customers, and to remain viable in an increasingly technology-based world. The role of information systems development has evolved from a business support role to a fundamental business driver where failure to utilize and leverage technological and human assets can cripple organizations. In light of historically dismal success rates for IT projects, organizational leaders must be willing to evaluate and implement methods to help IT project leaders effectively manage software development projects. Many different SDMs are available for use in IT software development projects and while empirical research supports their use, many organizations are resistant to adopting SDMs.

Organizations must also be cognizant of factors that can cause decreases in job satisfaction for IT personnel, which, in turn, can cause increases in voluntary turnover. The current study was designed to examine the relation between SDM use, leadership style, and job satisfaction. Although the results did not indicate a statistically significant correlation exists between overall SDM use and job satisfaction, other information indicated that SDM use paired with other factors, such as the number of team members for example, may result in significant correlation. The results of the study also indicated that in comparing groups of SDM users to non-SDM users, differences exist in levels of impact and significance for transformational leadership style and passive-avoidant leadership style.

Organizational leaders should use all information available to make better decisions for the overall health and viability of the organization. This research study may help organizational leaders identify strategies that result in an enhanced ability for IT project leaders to manage projects more effectively and efficiently. In addition to making decisions based on potential project success and user requirements, organizational leaders should also consider the needs of IT personnel who work in software development teams.

References

Aczel, A., & Sounderpandian, J. (2009). *Complete business statistics* (7th ed.). New York, NY: McGraw-Hill/Irwin.

Aditya, R., & House, R. (1997). The social scientific study of leadership: Quo vadis? *Journal of Management, 23*, 409-465. doi:10.1177/014920639702300306

Ahmar, M. (2010). Rule based expert system for selecting software development methodology. *Journal of Theoretical and Applied Information Technology, 19*, 143-148. Retrieved from http://www.jatit.org

Aken, A. (2008). CHUNK: An agile approach to the software development life cycle. *Journal of Internet Commerce, 7*, 313-338. doi:10.1080/15332860802250385

Ali, N., & Baloch, Q. (2010). Job satisfaction and employees turnover intention. *Interdisciplinary Journal of Contemprary Research in Business, 2*(5), 39-66. Retrieved from http://ijcrb.webs.com/

Amabile, T. (1997). Motivating creativity in organizations: On doing what you love and loving what you do. *California Managment Review, 40*, 39-58. Retrieved from http://cmr.berkeley.edu/

Ambler, S. (2010). 2010 IT project success rates. Retrieved from http://www.drdobbs.com

Amudha, T. (2010). Agile-Software development methodology. *Advances in Computational Sciences and Technology, 3*, 257-265. Retrieved from http://www.iasted.org

Ansari, M., Bhal, K., & Gulati, N. (2009). Leader-member exchange and subordinate outcomes: Test of a mediation model. *Leadership & Organization Development Journal, 30*, 106-125. doi:10.1108/01437730910935729

Ashrafi, N. (2003). The impact of software process improvement on quality: In theory and practice. *Information & Management, 20*, 677-690. doi:10.1016/S0378-7206(02)00096-4

Aurum, A., & Ghapanchi, A. (2011). Antecedents to IT personnel's intentions to leave: A systematic literature review. *Journal of Systems and Software, 84*, 238-249. doi:10.1016/j.jss.2010.09.022

Avison, D., & Fitzgerald, G. (1995). *Informations systems development: Methodologies, techniques, and tools*. Maidenhead, England: McGraw-Hill.

Avison, D., & Fitzgerald, G. (2003). Where now for development methodologies? *Communications of the ACM, 46*, 79-82. doi:10.1145/602421.602423

Avison, D., & Fitzgerald, G. (2008). *Information systems development: Methodologies, techniques and tools* (4th ed.). London, England: McGraw-Hill.

Avolio, B., & Bass, B. (Eds.). (1994). *Improving organizational effectiveness through transformational leadership*. Thousand Oaks, CA: Sage.

Avolio, B., & Bass, B. (2004). *Multifactor leadership questionnaire: Manual and sample set*. Retrieved from http://www.mindgarden.com

Aydin, M., Harmsen, F., Stegwee, R., & van Slooten, K. (2005). On the adaption of an Agile information systems development methodology. *Journal of Database Management, 16*(4), 24-40. doi:10.4018/jdm.2005100102

Baddoo, N., Beecham, S., Hall, T., Robinson, H., & Sharp, H. (2008a). Motivation in software engineering: A systematic literature review. *Information and Software Technology, 50*, 860-878. doi:10.1016/j.infsof.2007.09.004

Baddoo, N., Beecham, S., Hall, T., Robinson, H., & Sharp, H. (2008b). What do we know about developer motivation? *IEEE Software, 8*, 92-94. doi:10.1109/MS.2008.105

Baddoo, N., & Hall, T. (2002). Motivators of software process improvement: An analysis of practitioners' views. *Journal of Systems and Software, 62*, 85-96. doi:10.1016/S0164-1212(01)00125-X

Bajec, M., & Vavpotic, D. (2009). An approach for concurrent evaluation of technical and social aspects of software development methodologies. *Information and Software Technology, 51*, 528-545. doi:10.1016/j.infsof.2008.06.001

Bakker-Pieper, A., & de Vries, R. (2009). Leadership = communication? The relations of leaders' communication styles with leadership styles, knowledge sharing and leadership outcomes. *Journal of Business Psychology, 25*, 367-382. doi:10.1007/s10869-009-9140-2

Balsley, H. (1992). *Quantitative research methods for business and economics*. New York, NY: Random House.

Baskerville, R., Madsen, S., & Pries-Heje, J. (2011). Post-agility: What follows a decade of agility? *Information and Software Technology, 53*, 543-555. doi:10.1016/j.infsof.2010.10.010

Bass, B., & Avolio, B. (1990). *The multifactor leadership questionnaire*. Palo Alto, CA: Consulting Psychologists Press.

Bass, B., & Riggio, R. (2006). *Transformational leadership* (2nd ed.). Mahwah, NJ: Erlbaum.

Benbya, H., & McKelvey, B. (2006). Toward a complexity theory of information systems development. *Information Technology & People, 19*, 12-34. doi:10.1108/09593840610649952

Berger, H., & Beynon-Davies, P. (2009). The utility of rapid application development in large-scale complex projects. *Information Systems Journal, 19*, 549-570. doi:10.1111/j.1365-2575.2009.00329.x

Bertalanffy, L. (1968). *General system theory: Foundations, developments, applications* (Rev. ed.). New York, NY: George Braziller.

Beynon-Davies, P., & Holmes, S. (2002). Design breakdowns, scenarios, and rapid application development. *Information and Software Technology, 44*, 579-592. doi:10.1016/S0950-5849(02)00078-2

Bjorklund, T. (2010). Enhancing creative knowledge-work: Challenges and points of leverage. *International Journal of Managing Projects in Business, 3*, 517-525. doi:10.1108/17538371011056110

Bliss, W. (2010). Cost of employee turnover. Retrieved from http://isquare.com/turnover.cfm

Boban, M., Pozgaj, Z., & Sertic, H. (2007). Effective information systems development as a key to successful enterprise. *Management, 12*, 65-86. Retrieved from http://www.efst.hr/management/

Bodla, M., & Nawaz, M. (2010). Transformational leadership style and its relationship with satisfaction. *Interdisciplinary Journal of Contemprary Research in Business, 2*, 370-381. Retrieved from http://ijcrb.webs.com/

Boehm, B. (1988). A spiral model of software development and enhancement. *Computer, 21*(5), 61-72. doi:10.1145/12944.12948

Boener, S., Eisenbiss, S., & Knippenberg, D. (2008). Transformational leadership and team innovation: Integrating team climate principles. *Journal of Applied Psychology, 93*, 1438-1446. doi:10.1037/a0012716

Bonner, N. (2010). Predicting leadership success in agile environments: An inquiring systems approach. *Acadamy of Information and Management Sciences Journal, 13*(2), 83-103. Retrieved from http://www.alliedacademies.org/public/journals/Journals.aspx

Bono, J., Dzieweczynski, J., & Purvanova, R. (2006). Transformational leadership, job characterisitcs, and organizational citizenship performance. *Human Performance, 19*, 1-22. doi:10.1207/s15327043hup1901_1

Bono, J., Judge, T., & Locke, E. (2000). Personality and job satisfaction: The mediating role of job characteristics. *Journal of Applied Psychology, 85*, 237-249. doi:10.1037//0021-9010.85.2.237

Bostrom, R., Chin, W., & Gopal, A. (1993). Applying adaptive structuration theory to investigate the process of group systems support use. *Journal of Management Information Systems, 9*(3), 45-69. Retrieved from http://www.jmis-web.org/

Bostrom, R., & Heinen, J. (1977). MIS problems and failures: A socio-technical perspective, Part I: The causes. *MIS Quarterly, 1*(3), 17-32. doi:10.2307/248710

Bowen-Thompson, F., DeCaro, F., & Decaro, N. (2010). An examination of leadership styles of minority business entrepreneurs: A case study of public contracts. *Journal of Business & Economic Studies, 16*(2), 72-78. Retrieved from http://www.dowling.edu/jbes/

Brief, A. (1998). *Attitudes in and around organizations*. Thousand Oaks, CA: Sage.

Brief, A., & Weiss, H. (2002). Organizational behavior: Affect in the workplace. *Annual Review of Psychology, 53*, 279-307. doi:10.1146/annurev.psych.53.100901.135156

Brinkkemper, S., Jansen, S., Jaspers, E., & Vlaandered, K. (2010). The agile requirements refinery: Applying SCRUM principles to product software management. *Information and Software Technology, 53*, 58-70. doi:10.1016/j.infsof.2010.08.004

Buchner, A., Erdfelder, E., Faul, F., & Lang, A. (2007). G*Power 3: A flexible statistical power analysis program for the social, behavioral, and biomedical sciences. *Behavior Research Methods, 39*, 175-191. doi:10.3758/BF03193146

Burns, J. (1978). *Leadership.* New York, NY: Harper & Row.

Calisir, F., Gumussoy, C., & Iskin, I. (2009, December 8-11). *Factors affecting intention to quit among IT professionals.* Paper presented at the IEEE International Conference on Industrial Engineering and Engineering Management, Hong Kong.

Cao, L., Mohan, K., Ramesh, B., & Xu, P. (2009). A framework for adapting agile development methodologies. *European Journal of Information Systems, 18*, 332-343. doi:10.1057/ejis.2009.26

Cegielski, C., & Rainer, K. (2007). *Introduction to information systems* (3rd ed.). Hoboken, NJ: Wiley.

Cervone, H. (2011). Understanding agile project management methods using Scrum. *OCLC Systems & Services: International Digital Library Perspectives, 27*, 18-22. doi:10.1108/10650751111106528

Chemers, M. (1997). *An integrative theory of leadership.* Mahwah, NJ: Erlbaum.

Chen, H., Jiang, J., Klein, G., & Liu, J. (2010). Task completion competency and project management performance: The influence of control and user contribution. *International Journal of Project Management, 28*, 220-227. doi:10.1016/j.ijproman.2009.05.006

Chen, L. (2007). Job satisfaction among information system (IS) personnel. *Computers in Human Behavior, 24*, 105-118. doi:10.1016/j.chb.2007.01.012

Cherns, A. (1976). The principles of sociotechnical design. *Human Relations, 29*, 783-792. doi:10.1177/001872677602900806

Cherry, S., & Robillard, P. (2008). The social side of software engineering: A real ad hoc collaboration network. *International Journal of Human-Computer Studies, 66*, 495-505. doi:10.1016/j.ijhcs.2008.01.002

Clegg, C. (2000). Sociotechnical principles for system design. *Applied Ergonomics, 31*, 463-477. doi:10.1016/S0003-6870(00)00009-0

Collins, J., & Tubre, T. (2000). Jackson and Schuler (1985) revisited: A meta-analysis of the relationship between role ambiguity, role conflict, and job performance.

Journal of Management, 26, 155-169. doi:155-169.10.1016/S0149-2063(99)00035-5

Collins, R., Green, G., & Hevner, A. (2004). Perceived control and the diffusion of software process innovations. *Journal of High Technology Management Research, 15*, 123-144. doi:10.1016/j.hitech.2003.10.001

Colquitt, J., & Piccolo, R. (2006). Transforming leadership and job behaviors: The mediating role of core job characteristics. *Academy of Management Journal, 49*, 327-340. Retrieved from http://journals.aomonline.org/amj/

Conboy, K., & Morgan, L. (2011). Beyond the customer: Opening the Agile systems development process. *Information and Software Technology, 53*, 535-542. doi:10.1016/j.infsof.2010.10.007

Couger, D., & Zawacki, R. (1980). *Motivating and managing computer personnel*. New York, NY: Wiley.

Cray, C. (2009). *Impact of system development methodology use on employee role ambiguity and role conflict* (Doctoral dissertation). ProQuest Dissertations and Theses database. (UMI No. 3379652)

Cresswell, A., Gil-Garcia, J., Luna-Reyes, L., & Zhang, J. (2005). Information systems development as emergent socio-technical change: A practice approach. *European Journal of Information Systems, 14*, 93-105. doi:10.1057/palgrave.ejis.3000524

Creswell, J. (2007). *Qualitative inquiry & research design: Choosing among five approaches* (2nd ed.). Thousand Oaks, CA: Sage.

Creswell, J. (2009). *Research design: Qualitative, quantitative, and mixed methods approaches* (3rd ed.). Thousand Oaks, CA: Sage.

Creswell, J., & Plano Clark, V. (2007). *Designing and conducting mixed methods research*. Thousand Oaks, CA: Sage.

Dahiya, D., & Jain, P. (2010). Enterprise systems development: Impact of various software development methodologies. *International Journal of Advancements in Computing Technology, 2*(4). doi:10.4156/ijact.vol2.issue4.8

D'Andrea, V., Gangadharan, G., Ivanyukovich, A., & Marchese, M. (2005). Towards a service-oriented development methodology. *Journal of Integrated Design & Process Science, 9*(3), 53-62. Retrieved from http://www.iospress.nl/html/10920617_ita.html

Davis, F., Hardgrave, B., & Riemenschneider, C. (2002). Explaining software developer acceptance of methodologies: A comparison of five theoretical models. *IEEE Transactions on Software Engineering, 28*, 1135-1145. doi:10.1109/TSE.2002.1158287

Dawis, R., England, R., Lofquist, L., & Weiss, D. (1967). *Manual for the Minnesota Satisfaction Questionnaire*. Minnesota, MN: University of Minnesota.

Dearnley, P., Mayhew, P., & Worsley, C. (1989). Control of software prototyping process: Change classification approach. *Information and Software Technology, 31*(2), 59-66. doi:10.1016/0950-5849(89)90084-0

DeSanctis, G., & Poole, M. (1994). Capturing the complexity in advanced technology use: Adaptive structuration theory. *Organizational Science, 5*, 121-146. doi:10.1287/orsc.5.2.121

Duggan, E., Hale, D., Hale, J., Kacmar, C., & McManus, D. (2009). Software development methodologies in organizations: Field investigation of use, acceptance, and application. *Resources Management Journal, 22*(3), 16-39. doi:10.4018/irmj.2009070102

Dum dum, U, Lowe, K. & Avolio, B. (2002). A meta-analysis of transformational and transactional leadership correlates of effectiveness and satisfaction: An update and extension. In B. J. Avolio & F. J. Yammarino (Eds.), *Transformational and charismatic leadership: The road ahead* (vol. 2, pp. 35-66). Oxford, U.K: Elsevier Science.

Durham, C., Judge, T., Kluger, A., & Locke, E. (1998). Dispositional effects on job and life satisfaction: The role of core evaluations. *Journal of Applied Psychology, 83*, 17-34. doi:10.1037/0021-9010.83.1.17

Durham, C., Judge, T., & Locke, E. (1997). The dispositional causes of job satisfaction: A core evaluations approach. *Research in Organizational Behavior, 19*, 151-188. Retrieved from http://www.elsevier.com/wps/find/journaldescription.cws_home /714525/description

Eedara, V., & Korrapati, R. (2010, January 1). *A study of the relationship between software project success and employee job satisfaction.* Paper presented at the Allied Academies International Conference, New Orleans, LA.

Eterovic, Y., & Guerrero, F. (2004). Adopting the SW-CMM in a small IT organization. *IEEE Software, 21*(4), 29-35. doi:10.1109/MS.2004.3

Fields, K., Gibson, M., Ranier, R., Jr., & Roberts, T. (1998). Factors that impact implementing a system development methodology. *IEEE Transactions on Software Engineering, 27*, 640-649. doi:10.1109/32.707699

Fitzgerald, B. (1998). An empirical investigation into the adoption of systems development methodologies. *Information & Management, 34*, 317-328. doi:10.1016/S0378-7206(98)00072-X

Fitzgerald, G., Philippides, A., & Probert, S. (1999). Information systems development, maintenance, and enhancement: Findings from a UK study. *International Journal of Information Management, 19*, 319-328. doi:10.1016/S0268-4012(99)00029-8

Fleischman, G., Godkin, L., Kidwell, R., & Valentine, S. (2011). Corporate ethical values, group creativity, job satisfaction, and turnover intention: The impact of work context on work response. *Journal of Business Ethics, 98*, 353-372. doi:10.1007/s10551-010-0554-6

Frolick, M., Kloppenborg, T., & Tesch, D. (2007). IT project risks: The project management professional perspective. *Journal of Computer Information Systems, 47*(4), 61-69. Retrieved from http://www.iacis.org/jcis/

Gallivan, M. (2003). The influence of software developers' creative style on their attitudes to and assimilation of a software innovation. *Information & Management, 40*, 443-465. doi:10.1016/S0378-7206(02)00039-3

Ghazawi, I. (2010). Gender role in job satisfaction: The case of the U.S. information technology professionals. *Journal of Organizational Culture, Communications and Conflict, 14*(2), 1-34. http://www.alliedacademies.org/public/journals/JournalDetails.aspx?jid=11

Giddens, A. (1984). *The constitution of society*. Berkeley, CA: University of California Press.

Gottesdiener, E. (1995). RAD realities: Beyond the hype to how RAD really works. *Application Development Trends, 2*(8), 28-38. Retrieved from http://adtmag.com

Griesser, J. (1993). Motivation and information system professionals. *Journal of Managerial Psychology, 8*(3), 21-30. Retrieved from http://www.emeraldinsight.com/jmp.htm

Griffin, M., & Mason, C. (2002). Grouptask satisfaction: Applying the construct of job satisfaction to groups. *Small Group Research, 33*, 271-312. doi:10.1177/10496402033003001

Griffin, M., & Mason, C. (2003). Identifying task satisfaction at work. *Small Group Research, 34*, 413-442. doi:10.1177/1046496403252153

Guinan, P., & Sawyer, S. (1998). Software development: Processes and performance. *IBM Systems Journal, 37*, 552-569. doi:10.1147/sj.374.0552

Gumusluoglu, L., & Ilsev, A. (2009). Transformational leadership, creativity, and organizational innovation. *Journal of Business Research, 62*, 461-473. doi:10.1016/j.jbusres.2007.07.032

Hackman, R., & Oldham, G. (1975). Development of the job diagnostic survey. *Journal of Applied Psychology, 60*, 159-170. doi:10.1037/h0076546

Hanafiah, M., & Kasirun, Z. (2007). Using rule-based technique in developing the tool for finding suitable software methodology. *Malaysian Journal of Computer Science, 20*(2), 16. Retrieved from http://ejum.fsktm.um.edu.my/

Hannan, M. (2011). Analysis of the collaborative activities in software development processes from the perspective of chronotopes. *Computers in Human Behavior, 27*, 248-267. doi:10.1016/j.chb.2010.08.003

Hannon, J., & Westlund, S. (2008). Retaining talent: Assessing job satisfacton facets most significantly related to software developer turnover intentions. *Journal of*

Information Technology Management, 19(4), 1-15. Retrieved from http://jitm.ubalt.edu/

Hansen, B., Jacobsen, J., & Kautz, K. (2004). The utilization of information systems development in practice. *Journal of Information Technology Cases and Applications, 6*(4), 1-20. Retrieved from http://jitcar.ivylp.org/

Hardgrave, B., & Riemenschneider, C. (2002). Explaining software developer acceptance of methodologies: A comparison of five theorestical models. *IEEE Transactions on Software Engineering, 28*, 1135-1145. doi:10.1109/TSE.2002.1158287

Hekmatpour, S., & Ince, D. (1987). Software prototyping-progress and prospects. *Information and Software Technology, 29*, 8-14. doi:10.1016/0950-5849(87)90014-0

Herzberg, F. (1987). HBR classic: One more time: How do you motivate employees? *Harvard Business Review, 65*(5), 109-120. Retrieved from http://www.hbr.org

Highsmith, J. (2004). *Agile project managment: Creating innovative products* (2nd ed.). Boston, MA: Pearson Education.

Ho, L., Kuo, T., Lin, C., & Wu, Y. (2010). The factors influencing employees' attitudes in high-tech environment. *Industrial Management & Data Systems, 110*, 1054-1072. doi:10.1108/02635571011069103

Huang, A. (2009). A model for environmentally sustainable information systems development. *Journal of Computer Information Systems, 49*(4), 114-121. Retrieved from http://www.iacis.org/jcis/

Huisman, M., & Iivari, J. (2006). Deployment of systems development methodologies: Perceptual congruence between IS managers and systems developers. *Information & Management, 43*, 29-46. doi:10.1016/j.im.2005.01.005

Huisman, M., & Iivari, J. (2007). The relationship between organizational culture and the deployment of systems development methodologies. *MIS Quarterly, 31*, 35-58. Retrieved from http://www.misq.org/index.html

Hulin, C., Kendall, L., & Smith, P. (1969). *Measurement of satisfaction in work and retirement*. Chicago, IL: Rand McNally.

Iivari, J., & Iivari, N. (2011). The relationship between organizational culture and the deployment of agile methods. *Information and Software Technology, 53*, 509-520. doi:10.1016/j.infsof.2010.10.008

Jenkins, D., Salmon, M., Stanton, N., & Walker, G. (2008). A review of sociotechnical systems theory: A classic concept for new command and control paradigms. *Theoretical Issues in Ergonomics Science, 9*, 479-499. doi:10.1080/14639220701635470

Judge, T., & Larson, R. (2001). Dispositional affect and job satisfaction: A review and theoretical extension. *Organizational Behavior and Human Decision Sciences, 86*, 67-98. doi:10.1006/obhd.2001.2973

Jung, D., & Sosik, J. (2002). Transformational leadership in work groups: The role of empowerment, cohesiveness, and collective-efficacy on perceived group performance. *Small Group Research, 33*, 313-336. doi:10.1177/10496402033003002

Kahn, R., Quinn, R., Rosenthal, R., Snoek, J., & Quinn, R. (1964). *Organizational stress: Studies in role conflict and ambiguity.* New York, NY: Wiley.

Kaur, R., & Sengupta, J. (2010). A new approach to software development fusion process model. *Journal of Software Engineering & Applications, 3*, 998-1004. doi:10.4236/jsea.2010.310117

Kawalek, P., & Leonard, J. (1996). Evolutionary software development to support organizational and business process change: A case study account. *Journal of Information Technology, 11*(3), 185-198. doi:10.1080/026839696345243

Keller, R. (2006). Transformational leadership, initiating structure, and substitutes for leadership: A longitudinal study of research and development project team performance. *Journal of Applied Psychology, 19*, 202-210. doi:10.1037/0021-9010.91.1.202

Kempaiah, R., & Luftman, J. (2007). The IS organization of the future: The IT talent challenge. *Information Systems Management, 24*, 129-138. doi:10.1080/10580530701221023

Kendra, K., & Taplin, L. (2004). Project success: A cultural framework. *Project Management Journal, 4,* 30-45. Retrieved from http://www.pmi.org/Knowledge-Center/Publications-Project-Management-Journal.aspx

Khalifa, M., & Verner, J. (2000). Drivers for software development usage. *IEEE Transactions on Engineering Management, 47*, 360-369. doi:10.1109/17.865904

Kim, Y., King, W., & Ratbe, D. (1999). The fit between project characteristics and application development methodologies: A contingency approach. *Journal of Computer Information Systems, 40,* 26-33. Retrieved from http://www.iacis.org/jcis/

Kocheria, S., & Korrapati, R. (2010). A qualitative study on determining managerial styles for software development life cycle stages. *Proceedings of the Academy of Information and Management Sciences, 14*, 54-57.

Lambert, E., Hogan, N., & Barton, S. (2001). The impact of job satisfaction on turnover intent: a test of a structural measurement model using a national sample of workers. *Social Science Journal, 38*, 233-250. doi:10.1016/S0362-3319(01)00110-0

Lawler, J., Shi, K., Walumbwa, F., & Wang, P. (2004). The role of collective efficacy in the relations between transformational leadership and work outcomes. *Journal of Occupational and Organizational Psychology, 77*, 515-530. doi:10.1348/0963179042596441

Lawler, J., & Walumbwa, F. (2003). Building effective organizations: Transformationl leadership, collectivist orientation, work-related attitudes, and withdrawal behaviors in three emerging economies. *International Journal of Human Resource Management, 14*, 1083-1101. Retrieved from http://www.tandf.co.uk/journals/titles/09585192.asp

Lemons, M., Nath, R., & Parzinger, M. (2001). Examining the effect of the transformational leader on software quality. *Software Quality Journal, 9*, 253-267. doi:10.1023/A:1013763119819

Leonard-Barton, D. (1987). Implementing structured software methodologies: A case of innovation in process technology. *Interfaces, 17*(3), 6-17. doi:10.1287/inte.17.3.6

Lewin, K., Lippitt, R., & White, R. (1939). Patterns of aggressive behavior in experimentally created "social climates". *Journal of Social Psychology, 10*, 271-299. doi:10.1080/00224545.1939.9713366

Livermore, J. (2008). Factors that significantly impact the implementation of an agile software development methodology. *Journal of Software, 3*(4), 31-36. doi:10.4304/jsw.3.4.31-36

Loureiro-Koechlin, C. (2008). A theoretical framework for a structuration model of social issues in software development in information systems. *Systems Research and Behavioral Science, 25*, 99-109. doi:10.1002/sres.868

Mahapatra, R., Mangalaraj, G., & Nerur, S. (2005). Challenges of migrating to agile methodologies. *Communications of the ACM, 48*(5), 73-78. doi:10.1145/1060710.1060712

Marion, R., McKelvey, B., & Uhl-Bien, M. (2007). Complexity leadership theory: Shifting leadership from the industrial age to the knowledge era. *Leadership Quarterly, 18*, 298-318. doi:10.1016/j.leaqua.2007.04.002

Maslow, A. (1943). A theory of human motivation. *Psychological Review, 50*, 370-396. doi:10.1037/h0054346

Maslow, A. (1998). *Maslow on management.* New York, NY: Wiley.

Maurer, F., & Tessem, B. (2007, June). *Job satisfaction and motivation in a large agile team.* Paper presented at the XP07 Proceedings of the 8th International Conference on Agile Processes in Software Engineering and Extreme Programming, Como, Italy.

Maxim, P. (1999). *Quantitative research methods in the social sciences.* New York, NY: Oxford University Press.

McGregor, D. (2006). *The human side of enterprise: Annotated edition.* New York, NY: McGraw-Hill.

Miles, J., & Shevlin, M. (2001). *Applying regression & correlation: A guide for students and researchers.* Thousand Oaks, CA: Sage.

Millet, I., & Pinto, J. (1999). *Successful information system implementation* (2nd ed.). Newtown Square, PA: Project Management Institute.

Mishra, D., & Mishra, A. (2011). A review of non-technical issues in global software development. *International Journal of Computer Applications in Technology, 40,* 216-224. doi:10.1504/IJCAT.2011.039142

Mumford, E. (2006). The story of socio-technical design: reflections on its successes, failures and potential. *Information Systems Journal, 16,* 317-342. doi:10.1111/j.1365-2575.2006.00221.x

Nakata, C., & Zhu Z. (2007). Reexamining the link between customer orientation and business performance: The role of information systems. *Journal of Marketing Theory and Practice, 15,* 187-202.

Near, J., & Organ, D. (1985). Cognition vs affect in measures of job satisfaction. *International Journal of Psychology, 20,* 241-253. doi:10.1080/00207598508246751

Nelson, H., Nute, T., & Rodjak, D. (1996). Applying the spiral model: A case study in small project management. *Software Process-Improvement and Practice, 2,* 239-251. doi:10.1002/(SICI)1099-1670(199612)2:4<239::AID-SPIP55>3.3.CO;2-M

Niederman, F., & Sumner, M. (2004). Effects of tasks, salaries, and shocks on job satisfaction among MIS professionals. *Information Resources Management Journal, 17*(4), 49-72. doi:10.4018/irmj.2004100103

Nkenchor, C., & Ottu, I. (2010). Gender and leadership style as socio-demographic indicators of job satisfaction in Akwa Ibom state civil service. *Gender & Behavior, 8,* 2996-3016. Retrieved from http://www.ajol.info/index.php/gab

Northouse, P. (2004). *Leadership: Theory and practice* (3rd ed.). Thousand Oaks, CA: Sage.

Oriogun, P. (2002). Towards understanding software requirements capture: Experiences of professional students using the NIA to support the win-win spiral model. *Innovation in Teaching and Learning in Information and Computer Sciences, 1*(2). Retrieved from http://www.ics.heacademy.ac.uk/italics/

Orlikowski, W. (2000). Using technology and constituting structures: A practice lens for studying technology in organizations. *Organization Science, 11,* 404-428. doi:10.1287/orsc.11.4.404.14600

Ozer, M. (2008). Personal and task-related moderators of leader-member exchange among software developers. *Journal of Applied Psychology, 93,* 1174-1182. doi:10.1037/0021-9010.93.5.1174

Patnayakuni, R., & Ruppel, C. (2010). A socio-technical approach to improving the systems development process. *Information Systems Frontier, 12,* 219-234. doi:10.1007/s10796-008-9093-4

Pedrycz, W., Russo, B., & Succi, G. (2011). A model of job satisfaction for collaborative development processes. *Journal of Systems and Software, 84*, 739-752. doi:10.1016/j.jss.2010.12.018

Pickard, A. (2007). *Research methods in information*. London, England: Facet.

Pressman, R. (2007). *Software engineering: A practitioner's approach* (6th ed.). New York, NY: McGraw.

Rad, A., & Yarmohammadian, M. (2006). A study of relationship between managers' leadership style and employees' job satisfaction. *Leadership in Health Services, 19*(2), xi-xxviii. doi:10.1108/13660750610665008

Reynolds, G., & Stair, R. (2010). *Fundamentals of information systems* (5th ed.). Boston, MA: Course Technology, Cengage Learning.

Royce, W. (1970, August). *Managing the development of large software systems*. Paper presented at the IEEE Wescon, Los Alamitos, CA.

Royce, W. (1992). Status report: Computer-aided prototyping. *IEEE Software, 9*(6), 77-81. Retrieved from http://www.computer.org/portal/web/csdl/magazines/software#1

SamGnanakkan, S. (2010). Mediating role of organizational commitment on HR practices and turnover intention among ICT professionals. *Journal of Management Research, 10*, 39-61. Retrieved from http://www.macrothink.org/journal/index.php/jmr/

Sanchez, C. (2010). *Strategic management of the information technology resource: A framework for retention* (Doctoral dissertation). ProQuest Dissertations and Theses database. (UMI No. 3407444)

Sena, J., & Shani, A. (1994). Information technology and the integration of change: Sociotechnical system approach. *Journal of Applied Behavioral Science, 30*, 247-270. Retrieved from http://jab.sagepub.com/

Shore, B. (2005). Failure rates in global IS projects and the leadership challenge. *Journal of Global Information Technology Management, 8*(3), 1-6. Retrieved from http://www.uncg.edu/bae/jgitm/

Simon, M. (2006). *Dissertation & scholarly research: Recipes for success*. Dubuque, IA: Kendall/Hunt.

Singleton, R., & Straits, B. (2010). *Approaches to social research* (5th ed.). New York, NY: Oxford University Press.

Slusky, L. (1987). Integrating software modelling and prototyping tools. *Information and Software Technology, 29*(7), 379-387. doi:10.1016/0950-5849(87)90205-9

Spector, P. (1985). Measurement of human service staff satisfaction: Development of the Job Satisfaction Survey. *American Journal of Community Psychology, 13*, 693-713. doi:10.1007/BF00929796

Spector, P. (1994). Job Satisfaction Survey. Retrieved from
    http://shell.cas.usf.edu/~pspector/scales/jsspag.html

Spector, P. (1997). *Job satisfaction: Application, assessment, causes, and consequences.*
    Thousand Oaks, CA: Sage.

Standish Group. (2010). CHAOS manifesto: The laws of CHAOS and the CHAOS 100
    best PM practices. Retrieved from http://www.standishgroup.com/

Stogdill, R. (1974). *Handbook of leadership: A survey of theory and research.* New York,
    NY: Free Press.

Watson, L. (2009). Leadership's influence on job satisfaction. *Radiologic Technology,
    80*, 297-308. Retreived from https://www.asrt.org/

Westlund, S. (2007). *Retaining talent: Assessing relationships among leadership styles,
    software development job satisfaction, and turnover intentions* (Doctoral
    dissertation). ProQuest Dissertations and Theses database. (UMI No. 3288701)

Whitaker, K. (1997). Motivating and keeping software developers. *Computer, 30*, 126-
    128. doi:10.1109/2.562935

Wolff, G. (1989). The management of risk in system development: 'Project SP' and the
    new spiral model. *Software Engineering Journal, 4*(3), 134-142.
    doi:10.1049/sej.1989.0016

Appendix A: Request to Use Copyrighted Figures

Comments/Response to Case ID: 00629E13

Dear Jodine Burchell :

In response to your letter below, we are happy to grant you permission to reuse the IEEE copyrighted figures requested in all electronic and printed formats.

Our only requirements are that you credit the original source (author, paper, and publication), and that the IEEE copyright line (© [year of original publication] IEEE) appears prominently with each reprinted figure.

Sincerely,
Jacqueline Hansson, Coordinator

© © © © © © © © © © © © © © © © © ©
  IEEE Intellectual Property Rights Office
445 Hoes Lane
Piscataway, NJ 08855-1331 USA
+1 732 562 3966 (phone)
+1 732 562 1746 (fax)

IEEE-- Fostering technological innovation
and excellence for the benefit of humanity.
© © © © © © © © © © © © © © © © © ©

Greetings!

I am a graduate student at Walden University who is currently working on my dissertation. I have two items that I would like permission to reprint in my dissertation.

1. Figure 2. Spiral Model of the software process. From pg 64 of "A Spiral Model of Software Development and Enhancement" by B. Boehm, 1988, Computer, 21 (5).

2. Figure 2. Implementation steps to develop a large computer program for deliver to a customer. From pg 329 of "Managing the Development of Large Software Systems" by W. Royce, 1970, Proceedings of the IEEE WESCON, 26.

Of course, I will cite according to APA 6 and will print copyright information.

If you need any further information, I will gladly provide it as soon as possible.

Thank you!
Jodine Burchell
Doctoral Student Walden University

Appendix B: Text for Participants

CONSENT FORM FOR
"The Relationship between Software Development Methodology Usage, Leadership Style, and Job Satisfaction"

Dear Respondent,

You are invited to participate in a research study designed to examine the relationship between software development methodologies, leadership style, and job satisfaction. You were selected as a possible participant because you are considered IT personnel who have worked on a software development team (i.e. analyst, software designer, software development, software engineering, DBAs, QA, systems admin, etc.) in the past year and have knowledge and experience related to the topic. Please read this form and ask any questions you may have before acting on this invitation to be in the study. This study is being conducted by Jodine Burchell, doctoral candidate at Walden University.

Background Information:
The purpose of this study is to examine the relationship between the usage or non-usage of formalized software development methodologies for software projects, leadership styles of IT leaders, and the job satisfaction of IT personnel. The study will examine IT projects that are at least 2 months in length and having at least 4 team members. The study looks at software development methodology usage or non-usage from the perspective of their effect on IT employees' job satisfaction rather than the traditional focus of project success or user satisfaction.

Procedures:
If you agree to be in this study, you will be asked to take a brief electronic survey. The survey is anonymous and takes approximately 20 minutes to complete.

Voluntary Nature of the Study:
Your participation in this study is strictly voluntary. If you decide to join the study now, you can still change your mind during the study. Your decision whether or not participate will not affect your current or future relations with the institution in which you are employed. If you decide not to participate or discontinue participation, there is no penalty for doing so.

Risks and Benefits of Being in the Study:
Since respondent identification will not be collected, there is no risk that your answers will be connected to you in any way. There are no physical risks to you, nor is it likely that you will suffer any adverse psychological effects. Individual participants may benefit from this study to the extent that the findings provide information that is used by organizations in the development of strategies and managerial practices that lead to better quality of work life and improved job satisfaction of IT personnel.

In the event you experience stress or anxiety during your participation in the study you may terminate your participation at any time. You may refuse to answer any questions you consider invasive or stressful.

Compensation:
No compensation will be provided for your participation.

Confidentiality:
Any information you provide will be anonymous. No one, not even the researcher, will know who participated. Research records will be kept in a password protected media; only the researcher will have access to the records. All files will be destroyed five years following the completion of the study.

Contacts and Questions:
The researcher conducting this study is Jodine Burchell. The researcher's dissertation chairperson is Dr. Walter McCollum. If you have questions, the contact information is:

Jodine Burchell|406 Gwynn Ave|Murfreesboro, TN 37130|
Home Phone: 615-624-6248|Cell: 615-804-2238|
e-mail: jodine.burchell@waldenu.edu

Dr. Walter McCollum| Mobile: 571-215-3938|
e-mail address: walter.mccollum@waldenu.edu

If you want to talk privately about your rights as a participant, you can call Dr. Leilani Endicott. She is the Walden University representative who can discuss this with you. Her phone number is 1-800-925-3368, extension 1210. Walden University's approval number for this study is 06-22-11-0128057 and it expires on June 21, 2012.

You may print a copy of this informed consent statement for your records.

Statement of Consent:

By clicking "yes" below, you will be signing this form and giving your consent to take part in the current research study.

Clicking "yes" assures the following:

I acknowledge that I understand the nature of the study, the potential risks to me as a participant, and the means by which my identity will be kept confidential. My signature on this form indicates that I am 18years old or older and that I give my permission to voluntarily serve as a participant in the study described.

I understand the above statements and give consent for my information to be used in the study.
___yes ___no

Appendix C: Demographic Survey Items

1. I am at least 18 years of age.
   ___yes ___no   (thank and exit if the answer is no)

2. During the past year, I have participated in a software development team having at least 4 members for a software development project lasting at least 2 months.
   ___ yes ___no   (thank and exit if the answer is no)

3. Regarding your most recent software development project as described in question 1, what is the status of the project?

   ____finished ____ongoing

   - (If the project is finished) How long did the project last?
     - ___2 – 6 months
     - ___6 – 9 months
     - ___9 - 12 months
     - ___ over 12 months
     - ___over 24 months

   - (If the project is still ongoing) How long is the project expected to last in total?
     - ___2 – 6 months
     - ___6 – 9 months
     - ___9 - 12 months
     - ___over 12 months
     - ___over 24 month

4. How many team members did you have in total? ____ (thank and exit if less than 4)

5. What was your main position in the team?
   ___Project Leader
   ___Software analyst
   ___Software designer
   ___Software engineer
   ___Software developer
   ___Quality Assurance/Tester
   ___Database Administrator
   ___Systems Admin

___Other   Please specify_____

(thank and exit if position was project leader)

6. Did your team use a formal software development methodology? ___ yes ___no

7. If yes, which one?

___Waterfall

___Prototyping

___Spiral model

___Rapid Application Development (RAD)

___Capability Maturity Model (CMM)

___Agile Methods

___Object-oriented Design (OOD)

___Computer-aided Software Engineering (CASE)

___We used one, but I don't know the name of it

___Other please specify_____

8. What is your gender?

___female

___male

9. What is your age range?

___18-25

___26-35

___36-45

___46-55

___56 and older

10. How long have you been with your current organization?

___less than a year

___1-5 years

___6-10 years

___over 10 years

11. How many years of experience do you have in your current position?

___less than a year

___1-5 years

___6-10 years

___over 10 years

Appendix D: Receipt/Permission to Use the MLQ (5X)

The following order was placed with Mind Garden, Inc. Your order contains at least one PDF product. You will receive a separate e-mail containing instructions on how to access PDFs. If the e-mail does not appear in your inbox within 3-4 hours, be sure to check your Spam and Junk E-mail folders. Alternatively, go to www.mindgarden.com. At the top, click on Transform. In the green box, enter your 'ship to' email address from this order and create a password. Log in and access your products. (If you have previously created a Transform account for that email address, simply log in.)

We appreciate your business. If you have any questions about your order please contact us by either replying to this e-mail or calling our office at 1-650-322-6300.

Sales Receipt for Order 16239
Placed on Saturday, April 16, 2011 at 3:13 pm (PDT)

Ship To:
JODINE BURCHELL
Walden University
jodi_burchell@yahoo.com

Bill To:
JODINE BURCHELL
Walden University
jodi_burchell@yahoo.com

Product	Code	Quantity	Price/Each	Total
MLQ Reproduction Licenses 150 licenses (PDF)	MLQ-B-150-PDF	1	$135.00	$135.00

Shipping: Online Product Delivery: $0.00

Sales Tax: $0.00

Order Total: $135.00

This order has been paid in full

Appendix E: Permission Granted to Use JSS

Dear Jodine:

You have my permission to use the JSS in your research. You can find details about the scale in the Scales section of my website. I allow free use for noncommercial research and teaching purposes in return for sharing of results. This includes student theses and dissertations, as well as other student research projects. Copies of the scale can be reproduced in a thesis or dissertation as long as the copyright notice is included, "Copyright Paul E. Spector 1994, All rights reserved." Results can be shared by providing an e-copy of a published or unpublished research report (e.g., a dissertation).

Thank you for your interest in the JSS, and good luck with your research.

Best,
Paul Spector
Department of Psychology
PCD 4118
University of South Florida
Tampa, FL 33620
813-974-0357
pspector [at symbol] usf.edu
http://shell.cas.usf.edu/~spector

From: Jodine Burchell [mailto:jodine.burchell@waldenu.edu]
Sent: Saturday, April 09, 2011 1:13 PM
To: Spector, Paul
Subject: permission request

Dear Dr. Spector,

The purpose of this e-mail is to request your permission to use the Job Satisfaction Survey (JSS) to collect data for my dissertation research project. I am a doctoral student at Walden University in the Management program specializing in information systems management.

My research study will focus on the relationship between software development methodology usage, leadership style, and job satisfaction. The problem that this study will address is whether job satisfaction is influenced by the use of software development methodologies in IT projects. Contingent upon your approval, the JSS will be administered electronically via www.surveymethods.com.

I would be pleased to share the results of my study with you. Should you require additional information to render a favorable decision, please contact me. Thank you for your consideration.

Jodine Burchell

Walden University Doctoral Candidate

Curriculum Vitae

JODINE M. BURCHELL

EDUCATION

Ph.D. in Management, Information Systems Management
Dissertation Topic: The Relationship between the Use of Software Development Methodology, Leadership style, and Job Satisfaction
Walden University, Minneapolis, MN   Nov 2011

Master's in Computer Information Systems
University of Phoenix, Nashville, TN   2004

Associate's in Computer Information Systems
Nashville State Technical Institute, Nashville, TN   1997

Bachelor's in Business Administration
Middle Tennessee State University, Murfreesboro, TN   May 1988

ADDITIONAL TRAINING

Informix Training Courses, Chicago IL.   1998-2000
- Relational Database Design
- Developing Applications Using Informix 4GL
- Advanced 4GL Application Development

Faculty Training, Walden University   February 2009

ACADEMIC ONLINE INSTRUCTION EXPERIENCE

Lead Peer Mentor, Walden University   Dec, 2009 to current
- Serve as lead peer mentor to 30 doctoral level students in the College of Management.
- Utilize E-college and Live Meeting technology media to coordinate and facilitate biweekly doctoral student presentations.
- Review learning agreements and assist doctoral students with writing knowledge area modules (KAM).
- Facilitate a weekly cohort meeting for dissertation students to provide support, resources, and assistance in managing project timelines to achieve milestones while identifying potential risks as well as mitigation strategies.

- Provide students support and guidance with time management, answering questions regarding research, identifying and optimizing resources, and navigating through the doctoral process.
- Assist the faculty mentor and dissertation chair with the development of best practices in support of cultivating an online learning community and student-centeredness.

ACADEMIC INSTRUCTION EXPERIENCE

Online Adjunct Professor, Northcentral University   **April 2013 – present**
- MIS 7004 IT Data Communications Management
- MIS 7002 Database Administration and Management
- MIS 5002 Database Management Systems
- SKS 7000 Doctoral Comprehensive Strategic Knowledge Studies
- SKS 5000 Comprehensive Strategic Knowledge Studies
- MIS 7005 Enterprise Network Architecture
- MIS 5011 Computer Management Consulting

Online Adjunct Professor, Columbia Southern University   **March 2013 - present**
- DBA 8671 Technology and Innovation Management(Grad)
- DBA 8149 Business Research Methods(Grad)
- MBA 5401 Management Information Systems(Grad)
- BBA 3551 Information Systems Management
- ITC 3001 Personal Computer Fundamentals
- ITC 4760 Information Technology Evaluation and Implementation I

Hybrid Adjunct Professor, Vietnam MBA Program, CSU   **April – June 2014**
- MBAV 5401 Management Information Systems(Grad)
- MBAV 6961 Project Management(Grad)

Adjunct Professor, Strayer University, Nashville, TN   **March 2012 – present**
- CIS 105 Introduction to Information Systems
- CIS 170 Information Technology in Criminal Justice
- CIS 331 Spreadsheet Modeling
- CIS 500 Information Systems for Decision Making (Grad)
- CIS 515 Strategic Planning for Database Systems (Grad)
- CIS 542 Web Application Security (Grad)
- CIS 552 Cybercrime Techniques and Response (Grad)
- CIS 505 Communication Technologies (Grad)
- CIS 527 IT Risk Management (Grad)

Online Adjunct Professor, Everest University, Seattle WA   **April 2012-April 2013**
- CGS 2167 Computer Applications
- CGS 1280 Computer Hardware

PRACTICAL WORK EXPERIENCE

DelekUS, Brentwood, TN   **2012-present**
Senior Database Administrator
Database Security Administrator

- Experience working with and interfacing to database systems including Microsoft and SAP products.
- Self-starter, capable of learning new DBMS tools as required by the business.
- Perform database patching, upgrades and migrations
- Design and implement sophisticated HA, backup, recovery and DR solutions for mission critical databases.
- Technical expert representing the Infrastructure Group for database issues. Key resource to Applications Group during production problem resolution and performance enhancement.
- Responsible for development, testing, delivery, and configuration of all production databases. Ultimately responsible for data integrity and performance.
- Work with Software Developers to design database interfaces for new and existing applications. Provide mock implementations during development as needed.
- Strong communication skills in addition to a solid foundation of technical skills, analytical abilities, and knowledge of database design and architecture.
- Develops processes and procedures to enhance the stability and performance of database environment and service level support to users.

Ingram Periodicals Inc., LaVergne, TN   **1988 - present**
Advanced Programmer/Analyst

- Responsible for leading projects throughout the software development life cycle including gathering internal and external user requirements, performing needs analysis, creating design solutions, programming software, developing and implementing test plans, creating end-user and technical documentation, preparing training documents, and training end-users.
- Responsible for completing assigned programming tasks with accuracy and in a timely manner.
- Responsible for performing some database administration.
- Expert level experience in Informix 4GL-SE, SQL, and UNIX AIX. Some experience in Perl and Visual Basic. Exposure to C, C++, Oracle, FORTRAN, Assembler, Dbase, COBOL, and Pascal.
- Experience in all Microsoft Office products including Microsoft Project and Visio.

OTHER TEACHING/TRAINING EXPERIENCE

Ingram Periodicals Inc., LaVergne, TN
> Train end users for software rollouts
> Conduct periodic SQL training classes at corporate office

SCHOLARLY WORK: PUBLICATIONS IN PEER REVIEW JOURNALS

Quisinberry, W. & Burchell, J. (2013). Building collaborative learning communities: Support for peer mentoring models in online doctoral programs. *Mid-Continent Review, 2013*(2). p. 8-27.

Burchell, J. & Grizzell, B. (2012). Addressing the challenges of leading IT software development teams: The practical application of Transformational Theory vs. Complexity Leadership Theory. *Sheppard Journal of Practical Leadership, 6*(1). p. 1-13.

Burchell, J. (2011). Anticipating and managing resistance in organizational information technology (IT) change initiatives. *International Journal of the Academic Business World, 5*(1) p.13-22.

Burchell, J. (2011). Improving women's access to a globalized higher education: The promise of distance learning programs. Paper presented at the International Conference on Learning and Administration in Higher Education 2011. Abstract published in refereed conference proceedings. Nashville, TN.

Burchell, J. (2010). Anticipating and managing resistance in organizational IT change initiatives. Paper presented at the 6th Annual Academic Business World International Conference. Abstract published in refereed conference proceedings. Nominated for Best Paper award. Nashville, TN.

Burchell, J. (2009). The practical application of transformational theory vs. complexity leadership Theory on the challenges of leading IT software development teams. *Journal of Business and Leadership, 5*(1) p. 29-37.

Burchell, J. (2009). The practical application of transformational theory vs. complexity leadership Theory on the challenges of leading IT software development teams. Paper presented at the 5th Annual Business and Leadership Symposium. Abstract published in refereed conference proceedings. Fort Hayes University, Hayes, KS.

ACADEMIC AND PROFESSIONAL CONFERENCE PRESENTATIONS

Quisinberry, W. & Burchell, J. (2013). Building collaborative learning communities: Support for peer mentoring models in online doctoral programs. Paper presented at the 19th Annual Sloan Consortium, International Conference on Online Learning. Orlando, FL.

Burchell, J. (2010). Distance learning: A solid approach to improving women's access to a globalized higher education. Paper presented at the 7th Annual Yale Bouchet Conference on Diversity in Graduate Education. Yale Graduate School, Yale University, New Haven, CT.

Payne, A., Grizzell, B. & Burchell, J. (2010). Empirical study of diversity in online education: Management practices that promote women's access. Paper presented at the 16th Annual Sloan Consortium, International Conference on Online Learning. Orlando, FL.

PROFESSIONAL AFFILIATIONS

Sigma Iota Epsilon   Sept 2010 - present
- Member and currently serving on the Board of Directors as IT Director

Academy of Management   Dec 2010 – present
- Member and serving as Reviewer for the 71st annual meeting in San Antonio, TX

AWARDS

Walden University
- 2009 Honorarium - $300 awarded for presenting at a peer-reviewed conference
- 2010 Honorarium - $300 awarded for presenting at a peer-reviewed conference
- 2011 Honorarium - $300 awarded for presenting at a peer-reviewed conference